Dhyan Manik

Learning Thai

with

dâai ได้

Book I • Secrets 1–14

www.dolphinbooks.org

22 Secrets *of* Learning Thai

Copyright © Dhyan Manik 2018

Cover design and layout: by Uri Hautamäki / Data Graphics

Pictures of dâai ได้: Tone Artist

> Audio spoken in MP3 format by native speakers can be loaded from the following address:
>
> www.thaibooks.net
>
> Thai voice: Ms. Waree Singhanart
> English voice: Mr. Mark Harris

Publisher:
Dolphin Books
info@dolphinbooks.org
www.dolphinbooks.org

ISBN 978-9526651200

Acknowledgement

I would like to thank the following people for valuable guidance on Thai syntax and grammar, and assistance with editing and proofreading the text to reflect standard spoken Thai:

Ms. Duangmon Loprakhong, a Thai Teacher, Duke Language School, Bangkok

Ms. Waree Singhanart, a Thai Teacher, Bangkok

Mr. Kachen Tansiri, Kasetsart University, Bangkok

Mr. Watit Pumyoo, Chiang Mai University, Chiang Mai

I am also grateful to Mr. Mark Harris (British English) and to Mr. Walter Kassela (American English) for editing and proofreading the English text.

With the help of the above people, the clarity of the written Thai and English text has been significantly improved.

Table of Contents

Introduction 10
Transliteration and translation 12
Grammatical terms used in this book 12
Welcome to the world of dâai ได้ 15

1. dâai ได้ as a main verb 17

Secret 1 18
   A. Sentences with dâai ได้ before concrete nouns 20
   B. Highlights 21
   C. Understanding dâai ได้ 22
   D. Conclusion 23
   E. Language hints 24
   F. Simple advice 33

Secret 2 34
   A. Sentences with dâai ได้ before abstract nouns 36
   B. Highlights 37
   C. Understanding dâai ได้ 39
   D. Conclusion 39
   E. Language hints 40
   F. Simple advice 47

2. dâai ได้ as a helping verb 49

Secret 3 50
   A. Sentences with dâai ได้ after the main verb 52
   B. Highlights 53
   C. Understanding dâai ได้ 55
   D. Conclusion 56
   E. Language hints 57
   F. Simple advice 59

Secret 4 62
   A. Sentences with dâai ได้ and adjectives 64
   B. Highlights 66
   C. Understanding dâai ได้ 69
   D. Conclusion 70
   E. Language hints 72
   F. Simple advice 80

Secret 5 82
   A. Sentences with dâai ได้ before the main verb 84
   B. Highlights 86
   C. Understanding dâai ได้ 90
   D. Conclusion 95
   E. Language hints 97
   F. Simple advice 99

Secret 6 102
   A. Sentences with dâai ได้ and special verbs 104
   B. Highlights 105
   C. Understanding dâai ได้ 108
   D. Conclusion 109
   E. Language hints 110
   F. Simple advice 118

3. dâai ได้ and idiomatic expressions 121

Secret 7 122
   A. Sentences with dâai ได้ and idiomatic expressions I 124
   B. Highlights 125
   C. Understanding dâai ได้ 126
   D. Conclusion 127
   E. Language hints 128
   F. Simple advice 132

Secret 8 134
    A. Sentences with dâai ได้ and idiomatic expressions II 136
    B. Highlights 138
    C. Understanding dâai ได้ 139
    D. Conclusion 141
    E. Language hints 142
    F. Simple advice 146

4. dâai ได้ and asking permission and giving permission 149

Secret 9 150
    A. Sentences with dâai ได้
        asking for permission and questions 152
    B. Highlights 154
    C. Understanding dâai ได้ and asking for permission 157
    D. Conclusion 158
    E. Language hints 160
    F. Simple advice 165

Secret 10 166
    A. Sentences with dâai ได้ giving permission 168
    B. Highlights 169
    C. Understanding dâai ได้ 170
    D. Conclusion 171
    E. Language hints 172
    F. Simple advice 175

5. dâai ได้ with mental and physical actions 177

Secret 11 178
    A. Sentences with dâai ได้, wăi ไหว and pen เป็น referring to mental actions .. 180
    B. Highlights 182
    C. Understanding dâai ได้ 185
    D. Conclusion 187

    E. Language hints.. 188
    F. Simple advice 196

Secret 12 198
    A. Sentences with dâai ได้, wăi ไหว and pen เป็น referring to physical
       actions 200
    B. Highlights... 202
    C. Understanding dâai ได้ 206
    D. Conclusion 208
    E. Language hints..210
    F. Simple advice 215

6. dâai ได้ and negative actions 217

Secret 13 218
    A. Sentences with mâi-dâai ไม่ ได้
       mâi-pen ไม่ เป็น and mâi-wăi ไม่ ไหว
       when placed after the action verb.. 220
    B. Highlights..221
    C. Understanding mâi-dâai ไม่ ได้ 225
    D. Conclusion 227
    E. Language hints... 228
    F. Simple advice 233

Secret 14 236
    A. Sentences with mâi-dâai ไม่ ได้ before the main verb 238
    B. Highlights.. 240
    C. Understanding mâi-dâai ไม่ ได้ 243
    D. Conclusion 245
    E. Language hints... 246
    F. Simple advice 253

A. Introduction to sounds and Thai transliteration 256
B. Summary of some useful grammar terms 275

Contents of the Book II

Learning Thai Tenses with dâai ได้ • Secrets 15–22

In the Book II, which is a separate book, we shall learn in detail how to use Thai tenses.

- **Secret 15 – Basic phrase**
  The basic phrase doesn't have any time words, tense markers or any other indicators which would indicate the correct tense.

- **Secret 16 – Simple time words**
  Simple time words refer to a particular time – present, past or future.

- **Secret 17 – Time words of frequency**
  The time words of frequency tell how often something happens – present, past or future.

- **Secret 18 – Time indicators**
  The time indicators such as **lɛ́ɛu** แล้ว *already, state* or *condition reached* and **yùu** อยู่ *state exists* are used as indicators to emphasize the relevant action, state or condition – present, past or future.

- **Secret 19 – Present tense markers**
  The present tense markers such as **kamlang** กำลัง and **yùu** อยู่ are used for actions which are happening at the time of speaking.

- **Secret 20 – Past tense markers**
  The past tense markers such as **khəəi** เคย *once, used to* and **phɯ̂ŋ** เพิ่ง *just* are used to make it clear that the action has happened in the past.

- **Secret 21 – Future tense marker**
  Thai people use **tsà** จะ in a hypothetical manner to talk about possible future actions.

- **Secret 22 – Direction verbs**
  Direction verbs such as **maa** มา *to come* and **pai** ไป *to go* are used to express the direction of an action and also the correct tense.

BOOK I
SECRETS 1-14

Introduction

In this book (Book I, Secrets 1–14), we shall get to know **dâai** ได้ and learn different ways to use it in sentences. In the next book (Book II, Secrets 15–22), we shall review the Thai tenses in detail and compare them with English tenses.

Since the focus of this book is on **dâai** ได้, we try to use this beautiful Thai word in all sentences whenever possible. We have decided to talk about tenses even though there are no tenses as such in Thai. Tenses in Thai are expressed differently compared to English. When we use the word tense, we refer to the actual tense in English and also to the Thai way to talk about the present, past or future time.

Thai people use the word dâai ได้ daily in many different ways. If you learn to use this word well, your Thai language skills will take a quantum leap forward.

In this book, we have divided each Secret/chapter into six main sections. Section A consists of recorded sentences (English/Thai) using dâai ได้. In Highlights section B, we explain the structure and the meaning of the sentences used in section A. Section C is an attempt to understand dâai ได้ with regard to that particular topic. In section D we give a conclusion and grammatical summary of what we have learned. In language hints section E, we give more examples of dâai ได้ and sometimes point out other important aspects of the Thai language which are not directly related to the word dâai ได้. Lastly, in section F, we give simple advice on how to use dâai ได้ in everyday life with your Thai friends.

As a *main verb* before the noun, the meaning of dâai ได้ is simply *to get, to receive, to obtain*. It is used in a similar way to the English verb *to get*. dâai ได้ also has several other meanings depending on where it stands in the sentence.

When dâai ได้ comes *after the main verb*, it is usually placed at the end of the sentence. In that case, it plays the role of a helping verb expressing meanings like *can, being able to* or *being permitted to.*

dâai ได้ can also be placed *before the main verb,* in which case the meaning is *"getting"* the action in question or *to get an opportunity* or *a chance to do something.*

In addition, dâai ได้ is often used together with other words *in an idiomatic way* to express *a variety of different meanings.*

> Thai people use **dâai** ได้ in an intuitive way in a number of different situations to express feelings, wishes, and particular nuances while communicating with each other every day. Whenever you see **dâai** ได้ in a sentence, it always brings some additional flavour to the overall meaning. **dâai** ได้ is a very important word and it deserves a whole book. If you learn this word well, you will be rewarded.

We have decided to give the word **dâai** ได้ a face and name as a Thai girl, **dâai** ได้. That way the word **dâai** ได้ becomes more alive. Learning becomes a bit more fun and perhaps also easier.

dâai ได้ is a very beautiful and smart young girl. Pay attention to how she moves about in different situations. She can adapt herself very easily and plays several major and minor roles while interacting with other people.

You will see that she is quite a sophisticated person and is not always easy to understand. But one thing is sure, she is a lot of fun.

Transliteration and translation

> When we translate sentences in this book, we give two different translations. First, the correct English translation. We also give a literal word for word translation in English; then, all the words are in the basic form. Using this method, you are hopefully able to follow the structure of the Thai language better. It may also help you to learn new words more easily.

In Thai script, words and sentences are usually written together without any spaces. We use spaces between the words in this book since it will be easier for the learner to identify individual written Thai words. Spaces between words in Thai are normally used instead of full stops and commas employed in English. Since we put spaces between words in order to help you to read Thai, we have decided to use the symbol (-) when necessary to clarify the meaning of the Thai sentence where English would use a comma or a full stop.

You would be well advised to get yourself acquainted with basic phonetics and Thai sounds, and how they are produced and transliterated. You will then find that learning Thai becomes much easier. To understand some basic phonetics does not apply only to Thai, but other languages as well. After all, almost all English dictionaries contain phonetic symbols of how English should be pronounced. A short presentation of Thai sounds, transliteration and phonetics is given at the end of this book.

Grammatical terms used in this book

The aim of this book is to teach how the Thai word dâai ได้ is used with other words in sentences. Whether this usage is called grammar, syntax, sentence structure or the Thai way, does not matter. Yet, it is beneficial for us to know some grammatical terms used in English in order to understand the word dâai ได้ and the Thai language.

> The grammatical terms chosen in this book are from the perspective of the Thai language. They are not, by any means, an attempt to describe the English grammar. We just need some terms to illustrate how words are put together in Thai and where they are placed in the sentence. We must use the English language in order to understand the structure and the syntax of the Thai language.

The native speakers of any language are not usually aware of the syntax or the structure of their own language. Yet, they are able to make grammatically correct sentences since they are born into the habit of using the correct language. They have absorbed the grammatical rules of their own language subconsciously while learning it as a child.

You may find it helpful to have a glance at the summary of the grammar terms at the end of this book.

In this book, we are learning Thai with dâai ได้. The "Language hints" in section E and the "Simple advice" in section F contain notes on Thai language and grammar that go beyond the usage of the word dâai ได้. These can sometimes be more general in nature. Enjoy dâai ได้ and the Thai language.

Welcome to the world of dâai ได้

ยิน ดี ต้อน รับ เข้า สู่ โลก ของ ได้

dâai says: "Hello! My name is **dâai**. **dâai** is my nick name given to me by my mother. I have eyes, ears and feelings. I am smart, and I can teach you Thai."

ได้ บอก ว่า – สวัสดี ค่ะ – ฉัน ชื่อ ได้ – ได้ เป็น ชื่อ เล่น ที่ แม่ ตั้ง ให้ – ฉัน มี ตา มี หู มี ความ รู้ สึก – ฉัน เก่ง และ สอน ภาษา ไทย ให้ คุณ ได้

dâai bɔ̀ɔk-wâa – sàwàtdii khâ – tʃán tʃɯ̂ɯ **dâai** – **dâai** pen tʃɯ̂ɯ-lên thîi mɛ̂ɛ tâng hâi – tʃán mii taa mii hǔu mii khwaam-rúu-sɯ̀k – tʃán gèng lɛ́ sɔ̌ɔn phaasǎa thai hâi khun dâai

dâai say that – Hello khâ – I name **dâai** – **dâai** be name-play that mother set give – I have eye have ear have matter-know-consciousness – I smart and teach language Thai give you can

1. dâai ได้ as a main verb
(dâai pen krìyaa làk ได้ เป็น กริยา หลัก)

One way to learn to understand **dâai** ได้ is to use it as a main verb. As a main verb **dâai** ได้ can be placed before concrete or abstract nouns.

Secret 1	dâai ได้ before conrete nouns (dâai kɔ̀ɔn sǎamaan-yá-naam ได้ ก่อน สามานยนาม) The meaning is *to get something concrete.*
Secret 2	dâai ได้ before some abstract nouns (dâai kɔ̀ɔn aakaa-rá-naam ได้ ก่อน อาการนาม) The meaning is: dâai ได้ *converts some nouns into verbs in English*

SECRET 1

dâai is a good hearted and kind person. **dâai** says: "We must understand that giving and receiving are important qualities in life."

ได้ เป็น คน ที่ ใจ กว้าง และ มี น้ำ ใจ – ได้ บอก ว่า – เรา ต้อง เข้า ใจ ว่า การ ให้ และ การ ได้ รับ เป็น สิ่ง สำคัญ ใน ชีวิต

dâai pen khon thîi tsai-kwâang lέ mii náam-tsai – **dâai** bɔ̀ɔk-wâa – rau tôŋ khâu-tsai wâa kaan-hâi lέ kaan-dâai-ráp pen sìŋ sămkhan nai tʃiiwít

dâai be person that heart-wide and have-liquid-heart – **dâai** says – we must enter-heart that matter-give and matter-get-receive be quality important in life

dâai ได้ *to get* before nouns

When **dâai** ได้ is used as a main verb and placed before a concrete noun, it is usually translated into English as *to get, to receive* or *to obtain* something.

A. Sentences with dâai ได้ before concrete nouns

1. To get a bag – dâai kràpǎu ได้ กระเป๋า

Yesterday, I *got* a new bag.

เมื่อวาน ฉัน ได้ กระเป๋า ใบ ใหม่
mûua-waan tʃán *dâai* kràpǎu bai mài
when-yesterday I *get* bag-piece new

2. To get a computer – dâai khɔɔmphíutɔə ได้ คอมพิวเตอร์

Next month, I *am getting* my first computer.

เดือน หน้า ฉัน จะ ได้ คอมพิวเตอร์ เครื่อง แรก
dɯɯan-nâa tʃán tsà *dâai* khɔɔmphíutɔə khrûuang rɛ̂ɛk
month-next I will *get* computer machine first

3. To receive a salary – dâai ngən-dɯɯan ได้ เงิน เดือน

I *received* my salary three days ago.

ฉัน ได้ เงิน เดือน สาม วัน ที่ แล้ว
tʃán *dâai* ngən-dɯɯan sǎam wan thîi-lɛ́ɛu
I *get* money-month three day that-already

4. To receive a message – dâai khɔ̂ɔ-khwaam ได้ ข้อ ความ

I *got* your message.

ฉัน ได้ ข้อ ความ ของ คุณ แล้ว
tʃán *dâai* khɔ̂ɔ-khwaam khɔ̌ɔng khun lɛ́ɛu
I *receive* item-matter of you already

5 Wanting to get books – yàak-dâai năngsŭɯ
อยาก ได้ หนังสือ

I *would like to have* three books.

ฉัน อยาก ได้ หนังสือ สาม เล่ม ค่ะ
tʃán *yàak-dâai* năngsŭɯ săam lêm khâ
I *want-get* book three copy khâ

B. Highlights

We have placed **dâai** ได้ here before a direct object that is a concrete noun. The meaning in English is *to get*. It can also be translated into English as *to receive, to acquire* or *to obtain*.

Consider the following:

1 When **dâai** ได้ as a main verb is placed before a concrete noun **kràpău** กระเป๋า *bag*, the meaning is *to get* or *to receive a bag*.

2 When **dâai** ได้ is placed before a concrete noun **khɔɔmphíutɤ̂ɤ** คอมพิวเตอร์ *computer*, the meaning is simply *to get* or *to receive a computer*.

3 When **dâai** ได้ is placed before a concrete noun **ngən-dɯɯan** เงิน เดือน *salary*, the meaning is simply *to get* or *to receive salary*.

4 When **dâai** ได้ is placed before a concrete noun **khɔ̂ɔ-khwaam** ข้อ ความ message, the meaning is simply *to get* or *to receive a message*.

5 When **yàak-dâai** อยาก ได้ is placed before a concrete noun **năngsʉ̌ʉ** หนังสือ bag, the meaning is *to want to get* or *to want to receive a book*. The verb **yàak** อยาก *to want* must always be followed by another verb, here **dâai** ได้. Sometimes, it is more natural to say in English *I would like to have* instead of *I would like to get*.

C. Understanding dâai ได้

Generally, **dâai** ได้ can be understood as expressing a positive state of affairs, something that is possible.

When **dâai** ได้ as a *main verb* is placed before nouns, the meaning in English is *to get, to receive, to acquire* or *to obtain* something.

Word order:

subject + **dâai** + noun = *to get something*

tʃán + **dâai** + **khɔɔmphíutə̂ə** = *I get a computer.*

The semantic meaning of **dâai** ได้ is usually defined by the context, by the other words it is used with and by the place where it stands in the sentence.

dâai ได้ can be put before nouns, before adjectives, before and after verbs. It can be used in an idiomatic way to express several different meanings. **dâai** ได้ has several different meanings depending on where and how it is used in the sentence.

For Thai people **dâai** ได้ is a single word, and they don't usually think of it having different semantic meanings since they understand **dâai** ได้ intuitively.

In this Secret, we have placed the verb **dâai** ได้ before a concrete noun. The meaning is simply *to get, to receive, to obtain* or *to acquire* in English.

D. Conclusion

> Key: When **dâai** ได้ is used as a main verb and placed before a concrete noun, it is quite easy to understand and to translate into English since it is used in the similar way as the English word *to get*.

1. Place **dâai** ได้ as a main verb before a concrete noun in order to express meanings like *to get* or *to receive* something. For example, **dâai khɔɔmphíutɜɜ** ได้ คอมพิวเตอร์ is translated into English as *to get a computer*.

2. A compound construction **yàak-dâai** อยาก ได้ is a very common way to express *wanting to get* something.

3. In Thai, tenses are usually understood from the context and from the time words like **tɔɔn-níi** ตอน นี้ *now*, **mûɯa-waan** เมื่อวาน *yesterday*, **dɯɯan-nâa** เดือน หน้า *next month*. A comprihensive review of how to express tenses in Thai can be found in the book II Secrets 15–22. We take the liberty to talk about Thai tenses even though there are no tenses as such in Thai. The term tense is a handy English way to talk about the present, past and future.

E. Language hints

A) There is another verb **ráp** รับ *to get, to receive* that has a similar meaning to **dâai** ได้. Sometimes, these two verbs are used together in a compound construction such as **dâai-ráp** ได้รับ to emphasize the act of receiving.

> The compound verb **dâai-ráp** ได้รับ *to receive* is used in the same manner as the verb **dâai** ได้. This kind of construction is a slightly more formal style of language but the meaning remains the same or very similar. The colour of the sentence is different, however.

The verb **ráp** รับ *to receive* may also be used alone and the translation into English would be the same or similar to **dâai** ได้ or **dâai-ráp** ได้รับ.

The verb **ráp** รับ is a kind of a blunt and direct way to express meanings like *to get, to receive*, *to obtain*. It is also considered to be a slightly more formal style of language compared to using **dâai** ได้.

However, the colour of the statement is quite different with **dâai** ได้ since it is more expressive in the sense that it shows the feeling of getting something that is usually desired. On the other hand, the verb **ráp** รับ, expresses the act of receiving something without much feeling.

Consider the following:

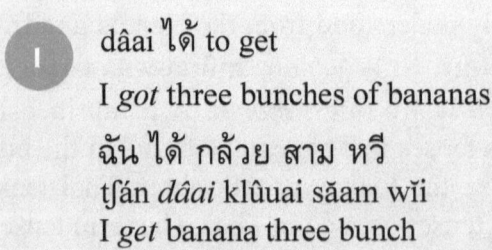

dâai ได้ to get

I *got* three bunches of bananas.

ฉัน ได้ กล้วย สาม หวี
tʃán *dâai* klûuai săam wĭi
I *get* banana three bunch

Secret 1

This is a simple expression when getting something with **dâai** ได้. The statement is expressing the act of getting.

> **2** ráp รับ to receive
>
> I *received* three bunches of bananas.
>
> ฉัน รับ กล้วย สาม หวี
> tʃǎn *ráp* klûuai sǎam wǐi
> I *receive* banana three bunch

This is also a simple and direct way, but the colour of the statement is slightly different. When we use **ráp** รับ *to get, to receive,* it is a blunt statement without the feeling of **dâai** ได้. Perhaps, there is an underlying understanding that bananas were free.

> **3** dâai-ráp ได้ รับ to receive
>
> I *received* three bunches of bananas.
>
> ฉัน ได้ รับ กล้วย สาม หวี
> tʃǎn *dâai-ráp* klûuai sǎam wǐi
> I *get-receive* banana three bunch

dâai-ráp ได้ รับ means *to get, to receive, to obtain.*

dâai-ráp ได้ รับ is a compound construction where two verbs have similar meaning. The colour of the statement is different compared to when **ráp** รับ or **dâai** ได้ is used alone.

This is a slightly more formal way to express the same meaning as the previous sentences 1 and 2.

B) **yàak-dâai**   อยาก ได้   *to want to get*
       yàak-dâai-ráp อยาก ได้ รับ   *to want to receive*

> The compound verb **yàak-dâai** อยาก ได้ *to want to get* can be placed *before a noun* but not before a verb. It must always be followed by a noun.

> **1**
>
> yàak-dâai อยาก ได้ to want to get
>
> I *want to get* three bunches of bananas.
>
> ฉัน อยาก ได้ กล้วย สาม หวี
> tʃán *yàak-dâai* klûuai săam wĭi
> I *want-get* banana three bunch

Wanting to get is expressed by the verb combination **yàak-dâai** อยาก ได้. This statement usually means that one is ready to pay for the goods that are being requested.

> **2**
>
> yàak-ráp อยาก รับ to want to receive
>
> I *want to receive* three bunches of bananas.
>
> ฉัน อยาก รับ กล้วย สาม หวี
> tʃán *yàak-ráp* klûuai săam wĭi
> I *want-receive* banana three bunch

The verb combination **yàak-ráp** อยาก รับ *to want to get* or *to receive* is very similar to the previous sentence 1. This statement is, however, a more blunt statement without the feeling of the verb **dâai** ได้. Perhaps, there is also an underlying understanding that one wants to receive free bananas.

> **3** yàak-dâai-ráp อยาก ได้ รับ to want to receive
>
> I *want to receive* three bunches of bananas.
>
> ฉัน อยาก ได้ รับ กล้วย สาม หวี
> tʃán *yàak dâai-ráp* klûuai săam wĭi
> I *want-receive* banana three bunch

The verb combination **yàak-dâai-ráp** อยาก ได้ รับ *to want to get* or *to receive* is a more formal way to express the same meaning as the previous sentences 1 and 2.

yàak-dâai-ráp อยาก ได้ รับ *to want to receive* can be used instead of **yàak-dâai** อยาก ได้ *to want to get*. The meaning is similar. Only the colour of the statement is different. This kind of construction is usually not used when speaking since it is very formal in style.

C) **dâai-maa** ได้ มา *to receive*

> Often Thais like to place the verb **maa** มา *to come* before the amount to emphasize the fact that one has received something.

> **1** dâai-maa ได้ มา to receive
>
> I have *received* three bunches of bananas.
>
> ฉัน ได้ กล้วย มา สาม หวี
> tʃán *dâai* klûuai *maa* săam wĭi
> I *get* banana *come* three bunch

maa มา *to come* is placed here before the number/amount and after the object, here **klûuai** กล้วย *banana*. **maa** มา emphasizes the fact of having bananas with her now.

This kind of structure is often translated into English as a present perfect tense, *has/have received*.

> **2** dâai-maa ได้ มา to receive
>
> I have *received* three bunches of bananas.
>
> ฉัน ได้ มา สาม หวี
> tʃán *dâai-maa* sǎam wǐi
> I *get-come* three bunch

If the context is clear the main object, here **klûuai** กล้วย *banana,* may be dropped.

> **3** dâai-maa ได้ มา to get
>
> Where did you *get* it from?
>
> คุณ ได้ มา จาก ไหน คะ
> khun *dâai-maa* tsàak nǎi khá
> you *get-come* from where khá

In Thai, when the context is clear, there is no need to mention the object. In English, we need to use the object *it*.

> **4** dâai-maa ได้ มา to get
>
> How did you *get* it?
>
> คุณ ได้ มา ได้ ยังไง
> khun *dâai-maa* dâai-yang-ngai
> you *get-come* get-how

Again, when the context is clear, there is no need to mention the object. In English, we need to use the object *it*.

5 dâai-maa ได้ มา to come

Whatever *comes* easy, goes easy!

ได้ มา ง่าย – เสีย ไป ง่าย
dâai-maa ngâai – sĭia pai ngâai
get-come easy – loose go easy

dâai-maa ได้ มา can also be used in idiomatic expressions as in the sentence 5.

D) There are several ways to say *I want* in Thai

yàak อยาก *to want* is put before verbs only

yàak-dâai อยาก ได้ *to want, to get* is placed before nouns only

au เอา *to take, to want* is placed before nouns only

tôrng-kaan ต้องการ *to need, to want* can be put before both verbs and nouns

Examples:

1 yàak อยาก to want

I *want* to go.

อยาก ไป
yàak pai
want go

Here, **yàak** อยาก *to want* is used alone. It is placed before the verb **pai** ไป *to go*. The verb **yàak** อยาก *to want* can be placed before verbs but not before nouns.

> **2** yàak-dâai อยาก ได้ to want to get
>
> I *want* ice cream.
> อยาก ได้ ไอติม
> *yàak-dâai* aitim
> *want-get* ice cream

yàak-dâai อยาก ได้ is translated into English as *to want* or *to want to get*.

While **yàak** อยาก *to want* is placed before a verb, the compound verb **yàak-dâai** อยาก ได้ *to want to get* is placed *before a noun* but never before a verb. Here **yàak-dâai** อยาก ได้ *to want* is placed before a noun, **aitim** ไอติม *ice cream*.

> **3** au เอา to want, to take
>
> I *want* this.
> ฉัน เอา อัน นี้
> tʃǎn *au* an-níi
> I *take* piece-this

au เอา *to want, to take* must always be followed by a noun.

au เอา means *to take*. It is often, however, translated into English as *to want*. **au** เอา alone can be put before a noun but not before a verb.

> **4** tông-kaan ต้อง การ to want, to need
>
> I *need to* go.
>
> ผม ต้อง การ ไป
> phǒm *tông-kaan* pai
> I *need-task* go

tông-kaan ต้อง การ *to want* can be followed by a noun or by a verb.

Here, **tông-kaan** ต้อง การ *to want* is placed before the verb **pai** ไป *to go*.

> **5** tông-kaan ต้อง การ to want, to need
>
> I *want* a new car.
>
> ผม ต้อง การ รถ คัน ใหม่
> phǒm *tông-kaan* rót khan mài
> I *need-task* car vehicle new

tông-kaan ต้อง การ can be placed before a noun or a verb.

Here, **tông-kaan** ต้อง การ *to want* is placed before the noun **rót** รถ *car*.

Sometimes, it is pointed out that **tông-kaan** ต้อง การ *to want, to need* is a more polite way to express *wanting*. It is, however, considered to be somewhat formal in style and is not used a lot by Thais in casual daily conversation.

> **E)** In Thai, it is quite polite to use **yàak-dâai** อยาก ได้ *to want to get* or **au** เอา *to take, to want* when stating a request. Particularly, if you place the polite request particle **khâ** ค่ะ or **khráp** ครับ at the end of the statement.

Examples:

> **1** I *take* three books. / I *want* three books.
>
> ฉัน เอา หนังสือ สาม เล่ม ค่ะ
> tʃán *au* năngsǔu săam lêm khâ
> I *take* book three copy khâ

Here, **au** เอา *to want, to take* is placed before the main noun, **năngsǔu** หนังสือ *book* and the classifier **lêm** เล่ม comes after.

This is considered to be a polite way to make a request in Thai. The polite way to say the same in English would be *I would like to have three books*. *I want three books* would be considered to be an impolite way to make a request in English.

Alternatively, we could use **yàak-dâai** อยาก ได้ *to want to get* or **tɔ̂ŋ-kaan** ต้อง การ *to want, to need* instead of **au** เอา *to want, to take*.

> **2** Dropping the main object
>
> I *want* three books.
>
> ฉัน เอา สาม เล่ม ค่ะ
> tʃán *au* săam lêm khâ
> I *take* three copy khâ

In this sentence, we have dropped the main object **nǎngsǔu** หนังสือ *book* and used only the classifier **lêm** เล่ม that here refers to books. The meaning is understood from the context.

F. Simple advice

> As a main verb, **dâai** ได้ *to get, to receive* or *to obtain* is used in a similar way to the English word *to get*. When **dâai** ได้ is used in this way, it should be quite easy to incorporate it into your daily speaking practice.

The difficulty arises from the fact that **dâai** ได้ can be put in several places in the sentence. It can be placed before nouns, before adjectives, before adverbs, before and after action verbs to express clearly different meanings. It can also be used in idiomatic ways to express several special meanings. In addition, **dâai** ได้ can be used in a compound construction with other verbs to convey specific ideas and meanings.

In this book (Book I), we shall introduce and discuss **dâai** ได้ when it is used in different places in the sentence and give you an idea how Thai people use it in everyday situations. Sometimes, the meaning is clearly different and sometimes there is only a slight difference in meaning. In the Book II, we shall discuss the Thai tenses in detail.

Secret 2

dâai likes many kinds of things and she likes very much to play as well. **dâai** says: "I feel uncomfortable and unhappy if life is not convenient, easy and fun."

ได้ ชอบ หลาย อย่าง และ ชอบ เล่น มากๆ – ได้ บอก ว่า – ถ้า ไม่ สนุก ไม่ สะดวก ไม่ สบาย – ฉัน จะ รู้ สึก อึด อัด และ ไม่ สบาย ใจ

dâai tʃɔ̌ɔp lǎai yàang lɛ́ tʃɔ̌ɔp lên mâak-mâak – **dâai** bɔ̀ɔk-wâa – thâa mâi sànùk – mâi sàdùuak – mâi sàbaai – tʃán tsà rúu-sùk ʉ̀t-àt lɛ́ mâi sàbaai-tsai

dâai like several kind and like play much-much – **dâai** say that – if no fun – no comfortable – no well – I will know-consciousness uncomfortable and no well-heart

dâai ได้ before abstract nouns

When **dâai** ได้ as a *main verb* is placed before abstract nouns, it sometimes turns a noun into a verb as far the English translation is concerned.

A. Sentences with dâai ได้ before abstract nouns

1. To be lucky – dâai-lâap ได้ ลาภ

Today, I *was* very *lucky*.

วัน นี้ ฉัน ได้ ลาภ มาก
wan-níi tʃán *dâai-lâap* mâak
day-this I *get-luck* very

2. Have heard – dâai-khàau ได้ ข่าว

I *have heard* that you have a new boyfriend.

ฉัน ได้ ข่าว ว่า – คุณ มี แฟน ใหม่
tʃán *dâai-khàau* wâa – khun mii fɛɛn mài
I *get-information* that – you have boyfriend new

3. To be touched – dâai-tsai ได้ ใจ

He is extremely skillful, he really *touches* my heart.

เขา เก่ง จัง – ได้ ใจ ฉัน มาก
kháu kèng tsang – *dâai-tsai* tʃán mâak
he skilful extreme – *get-heart* I very

3.1 Don't be *overconfident*!

อย่า ได้ ใจ
yàa *dâai-tsai*
do not *get-heart*

4. To smell – dâai-klìn ได้ กลิ่น

I *smell* something.

ฉัน ได้ กลิ่น บาง อย่าง
tʃán *dâai-klìn* baang-yàang.
I *get-smell* some-kind

B. Highlights

Here, we have placed **dâai** ได้ before an abstract noun.

> When **dâai** ได้ as a *main verb* is placed before an abstract noun, it sometimes changes a *noun into a verb* when translated into English. Abstract nouns describe things that cannot usually be touched or seen. In fact, in Thai it is the same structure whether we place **dâai** ได้ *to get* before a concrete noun or an abstract noun.

Thai people think in terms of *getting it* while English often think in terms *of being it*.

Consider the following:

dâai-lâap ได้ ลาภ *to get luck* is better translated into English as *to be lucky* or *having luck*.

lâap ลาภ *luck* is an abstract noun. When it is preceded by **dâai** ได้, it becomes a verb in English, *to be lucky*. Note that Thai people would think in terms of *getting luck*. **dâai-lâap** ได้ ลาภ in Thai it is usually associated with *money and winning in lottery* etc.

dâai-khàau ได้ ข่าว *to get* or *to receive information* is better translated into English as *to have heard*.

Here, **dâai** ได้ is placed before the abstract noun, **khàau** ข่าว *news*. It changes the noun into a verb in English, *to have heard*.

Thai people would think in terms of *to get* or *to receive information*, however.

dâai-tsai ได้ ใจ *to get heart* is better translated in English as *to be touched, to be impressed.*

tsai ใจ *heart* in this context is an abstract noun. When it is preceded by **dâai** ได้, it becomes a verb *to be impressed* in English. The younger generation (age about 13–30), particularly in Bangkok, often use this kind of expression and it can be considered popular slang.

When they say **dâai-tsai** ได้ ใจ, they mean that they are very impressed by someone who is really excellent at doing something. The literal translation would be *you get my heart*. In English, one could perhaps say in a similar situation *you are really excellent* or *you touch my heart.*

 yàa dâai-tsai อย่า ได้ ใจ *don't get heart* is better translated into English as *don't be overconfident.*

The original meaning of **dâai-tsai** ได้ ใจ is simply *to be overconfident*. In the past, the expression was often used with a negative connotation.

 dâai-klìn ได้ กลิ่น *to get smell* is better translated in English as *to smell.*

Here, **dâai** ได้ is placed before the abstract noun, **klìn** กลิ่น *smell*. It changes the noun into a verb in English, *to smell*.

Thai people would think in terms of *to get smell*.

C. Understanding dâai ได้

Generally, **dâai** ได้ can be understood as expressing the positive state of affairs, something that is possible.

When **dâai** ได้ as a *main verb* is placed before an abstract noun, it sometimes turns a noun into a verb as far as the English translation is concerned.

Word order:

subject + **dâai** + abstract noun = *verb*

tʃǎn + **dâai** + **lâap** = *I am lucky.*

When **dâai** ได้ is placed before abstract nouns such as **lâap** ลาภ *luck*, **oo-kàat** โอกาส *chance, opportunity etc.*, its semantic boundaries need to be extended to include the English verb *to be*.

dâai ได้ can change an abstract noun into a verb as far as the English translation is concerned. However, the Thai way to think about this is *to get* something. **dâai lâap** ได้ ลาภ *to get luck* is expressed in English *to be lucky*.

D. Conclusion

Key: In Thai, there is no difference whether you place **dâai** ได้ before a concrete noun like **kràpǎu** กระเป๋า *bag* or an abstract noun like **sìt** สิทธิ์ *authority*. Only the English translation is different.

Thai people are *getting* or *receiving* those things in the same way. It does not matter whether it is a *bag, luck* or *authority*. So, think as Thai people do! Then it is easy to understand.

1. However, if you need to translate into English, **dâai-sìt** ได้ สิทธิ์ would be best translated as *to be authorised* and **dâai kràpǎu** ได้ กระเป๋า would be *to get a bag*.

2. Sometimes, English uses the same kind of structure as Thai with abstract nouns. For example, **dâai ookàat** ได้ โอกาส can be translated into English as *to get an opportunity to*.

E. Language hints

Taste of **dâai** ได้ and more examples

A) Here are a few more examples of **dâai** ได้ being placed before nouns.

> The most simple way to use **dâai** ได้ is to place it before a noun, a concrete or an abstract noun.

> **1** Last year, we *got* a new car.
> ปี ที่ แล้ว เรา ได้ รถ คัน ใหม่
> pii-thîi-lɛ́ɛu rau *dâai rót* khan mài
> year-that-already we *get* car-vehicle new

dâai rót ได้ รถ means *to get* or *to receive a car*.

Here, **dâai** ได้ is placed before a concrete noun, **rót** รถ *car*. The meaning of **dâai** ได้ is *to get, to receive, to obtain*. See more on this in Secret 1.

> **2** I *was authorised* to go a for leave.
>
> ผม ได้ สิทธิ์ ไป เที่ยว
> phǒm *dâai-sìt* pai thîiau
> I *get-authority* go trip

dâai-sìt ได้ สิทธิ์ is translated into English as *to be authorised*.

Here, **dâai** ได้ is placed before a Pali/Sanskrit origin abstract noun **sìt** สิทธิ์ *authority*. The translation in English is *to be authorised*.

B) It is not always easy to distinguish whether the word is a concrete or an abstract noun, a verb or an adjective since adjectives can also play the role of a verb in Thai.

As far as the Thai language is concerned, this is not a problem. The difficulty may arise when we are trying to explain or translate the Thai structure into English. Similarly, we don't think in English that the word *fast* is an adverb in the sentence *he drives fast*. See more about how to make adjectives become adverbs in Thai in Secret 4.

Consider the following:

There are many ways to express *smelling* in Thai.

> **1** Passive smelling with dâai-klìn ได้ กลิ่น *to smell*
>
> I *smell* something.
>
> ฉัน ได้ กลิ่น บาง อย่าง
> tʃǎn *dâai-klìn* baang-yaang
> I *get-smell* some-kind

dâai ได้ is a verb. **klìn** กลิ่น *smell* is an abstract noun.

In Thai, we *get smell* and in English we *smell*. **dâai-klìn** ได้ กลิ่น *to smell* expresses passive smelling. **dâai-klìn** ได้ กลิ่น *to smell* means that smell is coming to you.

dâai-klìn ได้ กลิ่น is used for general smelling. It can be good or bad.

> **2** Active smelling with dom-klìn ดม กลิ่น *to smell*
>
> I *am smelling* something.
>
> ฉัน ดม กลิ่น บาง อย่าง
> tʃán *dom-klìn* baang-yaang
> I *smell-smell* some-kind

dom ดม is a verb. **klìn** กลิ่น *smell* is an abstract noun.

dom-klìn ดม กลิ่น is used in a similar way as **dâai-klìn** ได้ กลิ่น. However, **dom-klìn** ดม กลิ่น *to smell* means that someone *is actively smelling* something.

In this example, in Thai, *we smell the smell* (verb + noun) and in English *we smell* (verb only). The meaning of the statement is different from the previous sentence 1. Here the smelling is done actively. It is you who are smelling.

dom-klìn ดม กลิ่น is used for general smelling. It can be good or bad.

> **3** Active smelling with dom ดม *to smell*
>
> I do not want *to smell* this bird.
>
> ฉัน ไม่ อยาก ดม นก ตัว นี้
> tʃán mâi yàak *dom* nók tuua níi
> I no want *smell* bird body this

dom ดม *to smell* is a verb and can be used alone without a noun, **klìn** กลิ่น *smell*. **dom** ดม is used for general smelling. It can be good or bad.

dom ดม *to smell* is used for active smelling. It refers to the action of smelling. The meaning is the same as **dom-klìn** ดม กลิ่น *to smell*. The colour of the statement is a bit different.

The food *smells* delicious.

กลิ่น อาหาร น่า อร่อย
klìn aahăan nâa-arɔ̀i
smell food nâa-delicious

nâa-arɔ̀i น่า อร่อย *delicious* is an adjective that also plays a role of a verb here. We do not translate the prefix **nâa** น่า into English since there is no similar word in English.

Alternatively, the same can be expressed in Thai as:

Food *has* a delicious *smell*.

อาหาร มี กลิ่น น่า อร่อย
aahăan *mii klìn* nâa-arɔ̀i
food *have smell* nâa-delicious

klìn กลิ่น *smell* is an abstract noun. In English the word *smell* can either be a noun or a verb. This statement is simply describing how the food smells.

klìn กลิ่น alone is used for general smelling. It can be good or bad. This is just stating a general fact.

> **6** The ocean *smells* salty.
>
> กลิ่น ทะเล เค็ม
> *klìn* thálee khem
> *smell* ocean salty

khem เค็ม *salty* is an adjective that also plays a role of a verb here.

Alternatively, the same can be expressed in Thai as:

> **7** Ocean *has* a salty *smell*.
>
> ทะเล มี กลิ่น เค็ม
> thálee *mii klìn* khem
> Ocean *have smell* salty

Here, **klìn** กลิ่น *smell* is an abstract noun. This statement is simply describing how the ocean smells. It can be good or bad.

> **8** Flowers *smell* fantastic.
>
> ดอก ไม้ หอม จัง เลย
> dòok-máai *hɔ̌ɔm* tsang ləəi
> flower-plant *smell* very sure

hɔ̌ɔm หอม *to be pleasant smelling, something that smells good.*

This statement is simply describing how flowers smell.

hɔ̌ɔm หอม is an adjective that can also play a role of a verb in the sentence.

hɔ̌ɔm หอม is used for something that smells good such as perfumes, flowers, foods etc. It refers to objects that smell good. This word is not used for active smelling. It describes a state of *good smell*.

It *stinks*. It smells bad.

มัน เหม็น
man *měn*
It *stink*

This statement is simply describing how something smells or stinks. **měn** เหม็น is used for a *bad smell*. It refers to the objects that are smelling bad.

měn เหม็น is an adjective that also plays a role of a verb in the sentence. **měn** เหม็น means *to be bad smelling, something that stinks*.

C) The heart word **tsai** ใจ *heart, mind, spirit*

Earlier in this Secret, we introduced an expression where **tsai** ใจ *heart* was used with verb **dâai** ได้ *to get*, **dâai-tsai** ได้ ใจ *to be impressed, to be touched* by someone.

tsai ใจ *heart* is a very important word in Thai. It is used in many ways with a number of words to form a vast variety of different meanings.

Here are a few common sentences with **tsai** ใจ – heart word

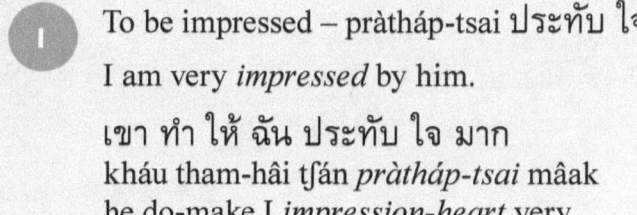

To be impressed – **pràtháp-tsai** ประทับ ใจ

I am very *impressed* by him.

เขา ทำ ให้ ฉัน ประทับ ใจ มาก
kháu tham-hâi tʃán *pràtháp-tsai* mâak
he do-make I *impression-heart* very

pràtháp-tsai ประทับ ใจ also means *to be impressed*.

This is a more common way to express the same meaning as **dâai-tsai** ได้ ใจ *to be touched, to be impressed* since **dâai-tsai** ได้ ใจ could be considered as a kind of semi-slang.

This sentence could also be translated into English as *he impresses me a lot*.

> **2**   To be happy – dii-tsai ดี ใจ
>
> I am very *happy*.
>
> ฉัน ดี ใจ มาก
> tʃán *dii-tsai* mâak
> I *good-heart* very

> **3**   Being good hearted – tsai-dii ใจ ดี
>
> He is a very *good hearted* person.
>
> เขา ใจ ดี มาก
> kháu *tsai-dii* mâak
> he *heart-good* very

> **4**   To trust – wái-tsai ไว้ ใจ
>
> He can *be trusted*.
>
> เขา ไว้ ใจ ได้
> kháu *wái-tsai* dâai
> he *keep-heart* can

5 To agree, to sympathize – hĕn-tsai เห็น ใจ

I *sympathize* with him.

ผม เห็น ใจ เขา
phŏm *hĕn-tsai* kháu
I *see-heart* with he

6 To go along – taam-tsai ตาม ใจ

Follow your heart.

ตาม ใจ คุณ
taam-tsai khun
follow-heart you

7 To be interested in – sŏn-tsai สน ใจ

I am *interested* in him.

ฉัน สน ใจ เขา
tʃán sŏn-tsai kháu
I *interest-heart* he

F. Simple advice

When **dâai** ได้ as a *main verb* is placed before *concrete nouns* such as *cars, apples, houses,* the meaning in Thai is *to get, to receive* or *to obtain.* See Secret 1.

> When **dâai** ได้ is placed before *abstract nouns* such as *luck, opportunity, happiness etc.*, it often turns the noun into a verb as far as the English translation is concerned.
>
> However, the Thai structure is the same for abstract and concrete nouns. It is only the English translation that may be different.

Thai people do not usually see any difference whether **dâai** ได้ is placed before an abstract noun or a concrete noun. Thais *get luck* and English *are lucky*. The meaning is the same.

dâai ได้ can also be placed as *a helping verb* before or after the main verb. In the next four Secrets 3–6, we shall have a look at these cases. It is very interesting to know how **dâai** ได้ is used as *a helping verb*.

2. dâai ได้ as a helping verb
(dâai pen krìyaa tʃûuai ได้ เป็น กริยา ช่วย)

One way to learn to understand **dâai** ได้ is to use it as a helping verb.

As a helping verb **dâai** ได้ can be placed before or after the main verb. The grammatical function and meaning are very different.

Secret 3   dâai ได้ as a helping verb after the main verb
(dâai pen krìyaa tʃûuai lăng krì-yaa làk
ได้ เป็น กริยา ช่วย หลัง กริยา หลัก)

The meaning is *can, being able to* or *being permitted to* do something.

Secret 4   dâai ได้ and adjectives
(dâai lɛ́ kham khunnásàp ได้ และ คำ คุณศัพท์)

When dâai ได้ is placed before an adjective, it turns an adjective into an adverb. *Beautiful* becomes *beautifully*. When dâai ได้ is placed after an adjective, it tells in what way someone *is able* or *permitted to* do something.

Secret 5   dâai ได้ as a helping verb before the main verb
(dâai pen krìyaa tʃûuai kɔ̀ɔn krìyaa làk
ได้ เป็น กริยา ช่วย ก่อน กริยา หลัก)

When dâai ได้ is placed before the main verb, it means "to get" the action in question. It can also be translated into English as *to get an opportunity to* or *a chance to* do something.

Secret 6   dâai ได้ as a helping verb with some special verbs
(dâai pen krìyaa tʃûuai lɛ́ krìyaa phísèet
ได้ เป็น กริยา ช่วย และ กริยา พิเศษ)

When dâai ได้ is used with some special verbs in the compound construction, it can change the meaning of the other verb.

Secret 3

dâai ได้ is a person who knows that some things can be eaten and some others can't because they are not good for your health. **dâai** ได้ says: "Drinks that have too much sugar are not good for you. Drinking alcohol every day is not good but eating fruit every day is good for your health."

ได้ เป็น คน ที่ รู้ ว่า อะไร กิน ได้ และ อะไร กิน ไม่ ได้ เพราะว่า ไม่ ดี ต่อ สุขภาพ – ได้ บอก ว่า – ดื่ม เครื่อง ดื่ม ที่ มี น้ำตาล มาก เกินไป ไม่ ดี – กิน เหล้า ทุก วัน ไม่ ดี แต่ กิน ผลไม้ ทุก วัน ดี

dâai pen khon thîi rúu wâa arai kin dâai lɛ́ arai kin mâi-dâai phrɔ́-wâa mâi dii tɔ̀ɔ sùkkhàphâap – **dâai** bɔ̀ɔk-wâa – dùum khrûuang-dùum thîi mii námtaan mâak-kəən-pai mâi dii – kin lâu thúk-wan mâi dii tɛ̀ɛ kin phǒn-lá-máai thúk-wan dii

dâai be person that know that what eat can and what eat *no-can* because-that no good to health – **dâai** say that – drink beverage-drink that have sugar much exceed-go no good – eat alcohol every-day no good but eat fruit-tree every-day good

dâai ได้ as a helping verb after the main verb

When **dâai** ได้ is placed after the main verb, it is usually translated into English as *can, being able to, being permitted* or *allowed to* do something.

Secret 3

A. Sentences with dâai ได้ after the main verb

1 I can drink – tʃán dùum dâai ฉัน ดื่ม ได้

I *can drink* this water.

ฉัน ดื่ม น้ำ นี้ ได้
tʃán *dùum* náam-níi *dâai*
I *drink* water this *can*

1.1 This water is *drinkable*.

น้ำ นี้ ดื่ม ได้
náam níi *dùum-dâai*
water this *drink-can*

2 He is allowed to eat – kháu kin dâai เขา กิน ได้

He *is allowed to eat* bananas.

เขา กิน กล้วย ได้
kháu *kin* klûuai *dâai*
he *eat* banana *can*

2.1 Bananas are *edible*.

กล้วย กิน ได้
klûuai *kin-dâai*
banana *eat-can*

3 Being able to speak – phûut dâai พูด ได้

I *can speak* English.

ฉัน พูด ภาษา อังกฤษ ได้
tʃán *phûut* phaasăa anggrìt *dâai*
I *speak* language English *can*

Secret 3

3.1 I *cannot speak* English.

ฉัน พูด ภาษา อังกฤษ ไม่ได้
tʃán *phûut* phaasăa anggrìt *mâi-dâai*
I *speak* language English *no-can*

4 Not being able to do – tham mâi-dâai ทำ ไม่ ได้

I am *not able to do* this work.

ฉัน ทำ งาน นี้ ไม่ ได้
tʃán *tham* ngaan-níi *mâi-dâai*
I *do* work this *no-can*

4.1 This job *can't be done*.

งาน นี้ ทำ ไม่ ได้
ngaan-níi *tham mâi-dâai*
work this *do no-can*

B. Highlights

Here, we have placed **dâai** ได้ *after the main verb*. It is simply translated into English as *can*. When **dâai** ได้ refers to an action that *is possible*, it is usually placed at the end of the sentence or statement.

When **dâai** ได้ is placed after the main verb, depending on the context, the English translation of the verb **dâai** ได้ includes verbs like *can, being able to, being permitted to* or *being allowed to* do something.

When **dâai** ได้ refers to the quality of a subject other than a personal pronoun, then it is best translated into English using an *adjective* or a *passive voice*. For example **kin-dâai** กิน ได้ is translated as *to be edible* or *can be eaten*.

Consider the following:

> **1** The sentence **tʃán dùum-dâai** ฉัน ดื่ม ได้ is translated as *I can drink* or *I am allowed to drink*.

The sentence **náam dùum-dâai** น้ำ ดื่ม ได้ is translated into English as *water is drinkable*. Drinkable is an adjective and refers to water. Water does not drink, but it *can be drinkable*.

> **2** The sentence **kháu kin-dâai** เขา กิน ได้ is translated as *he can eat* or *he is allowed to eat*.

The sentence **klûuai kin-dâai** กล้วย กิน ได้ is translated into English as *bananas are edible*. Bananas do not usually eat, but they can *be eaten*.

> **3** In the sentence **tʃán phûut phaasǎa anggrìt dâai** ฉัน พูด ภาษา อังกฤษ ได้, **dâai** ได้ refers to the mental ability, *being able to* speak English.

This sentence is negated as follows: **tʃán phûut phaasǎa anggrìt mâi-dâai** ฉัน พูด ภาษา อังกฤษ ได้ *I cannot speak English*.

> **4** **tʃán tham mâi-dâai** ฉัน ทำ ไม่ ได้ is translated as *I am not able to do* or depending on the context *I am not allowed to do*. In negative statements, **mâi** ไม่ *no* is placed before the helping verb **dâai** ได้.

The sentence **ngaan níi tham-mâi-dâai** งาน นี้ ทำ ไม่ ได้ is translated into English as *this job is impossible to do* or as a passive voice *this job cannot be done.*

C. Understanding dâai ได้

Generally, **dâai** ได้ can be understood as expressing a positive state of affairs, something that is possible.

> One way to understand **dâai** ได้ is to take note of whether it stands before or after the main verb. When **dâai** ได้ is placed after the main verb, depending on the context, it can be translated into English in several different ways.

When **dâai** ได้ is placed after the main verb, it is usually translated into English as *can* or *being able to* do something. **dâai** ได้ is also used in this way to express meanings like *being permitted* or *being allowed to* do something.

Depending on the context, **dùum-dâai** ดื่ม ได้ can also be translated into English as an adjective, *drinkable*. The Thai way to think about this is, however, *drink-can*.

Word order:

> Subject + verb + **dâai**
> = *can, being able, being permitted* or *being allowed to*
>
> tʃán + kin + **dâai**
> = *I can eat, I am able to eat, I am allowed to eat.*
>
> klûuai + kin + **dâai**
> = *Bananas can be eaten.*

When **dâai** ได้ is placed after the main verb, it plays the role of the helping verb and its semantic boundaries are defined by English words such as *can, being able to, being allowed to* or *being permitted to*.

When **dâai** ได้ is placed after the main verb, it is usually placed at the end of a sentence or statement.

D. Conclusion

> Key: The grammatical term for this type of auxiliary or helping verbs is a "modal verb". **dâai** ได้ is a good example. English, in similar cases, uses the helping verb *can*.

dâai ได้ and **mâi-dâai** ไม่ ได้ are used in the similar way as English verbs *can* and *cannot*. In Thai, when **dâai** ได้ or **mâi-dâai** ไม่ ได้ are placed after the action verb, they usually come at the end of the sentence while in English *can* and *cannot* are usually placed directly before the main verb.

1. Place **dâai** ได้ after the main verb, usually at the end of the sentence, in order to express meanings like *being able to, being permitted to* or *being allowed to* do something. It may help if you think in terms of the action being possible *whatever the reason.*

2. The negative term **mâi-dâai** ไม่ ได้ at end of the sentence is translated into English as *cannot, not being able to* or *not being permitted to.* The action is not possible *whatever the reason*. In this negative expression the words, **mâi** ไม่ and **dâai** ได้ cannot usually be separated.

3. Depending on the context, **dâai** ได้ can also be translated into English as an *adjective*. The phrase **klûuai kin-dâai** กล้วย กิน ได้ can be translated into English as *bananas are edible*. The Thai way to think about this is, however, *banana eat can, bananas can*

be eaten. The word **dâai** ได้ is a verb whatever the translation into English may be.

E. Language hints

There is another word in Thai that means *can* or *being able to*, namely **săamâat** สามารถ

It is used grammatically somewhat differently. While **dâai** ได้ comes after the main verb, **săamâat** สามารถ is placed before the main verb. **săamâat** สามารถ is often used in formal situations while **dâai** ได้ can be used in formal and casual situations.

Often, both **săamâat** สามารถ and **dâai** ได้ are employed simultaneously in the same sentence.

Examples:

1. This water *is drinkable*.
น้ำ นี้ สามารถ ดื่ม ได้
náam níi *săamâat dùum dâai*
water this *can drink can*

săamâat สามารถ *can* is put before the main verb **dùum** ดื่ม *to drink* and **dâai** ได้ *can* after the main verb. In casual speech, **săamâat** สามารถ is usually dropped.

2. He *can eat* bananas.
เขา สามารถ กิน กล้วย ได้
kháu *săamâat kin* klûuai *dâai*
he *can eat* banana *can*

săamâat สามารถ is placed before the main verb **kin** กิน *to eat* and **dâai** ได้ after the main verb. In casual speech, **săamâat** สามารถ is usually dropped.

> **3**
> I *can't do* this work.
> ผม ไม่ สามารถ ทำ งาน นี้ ได้
> phŏm *mâi săamâat tham* ngaan-níi *dâai*
> I *no can do* work-this *can*

In the negative sentence, the word **mâi** ไม่ *no* comes before the verb **săamâat** สามารถ and not before the word **dâai** ได้.

In casual speech, **săamâat** สามารถ is usually dropped. Then, however, the word **mâi** ไม่ *no* is placed before the word **dâai** ได้, **mâi-dâai** ไม่ ได้.

> **4**
> This newspaper *is readable*.
> หนังสือพิมพ์ ฉบับ นี้ สามารถ อ่าน ได้
> năngsŭɯ-phim tʃàbàp níi *săamâat àan-dâai*
> book-print copy this *can-read-can*

Often when we use **săamâat** สามารถ, it sounds more natural to include **dâai** ได้ with it. **săamâat** สามารถ is not often used alone. Why? It does not sound right! In casual speech, **săamâat** สามารถ is usually dropped.

> **5**
> I *remember*.
> ผม สามารถ จำ ได้
> phŏm *săamâat tsam-dâai*
> I *can remember-can*

tsam-dâai จำ ได้ *to remember* is one word and cannot usually be separated. This is a formal way to say *I am able to remember*. In casual speech, **săamâat** สามารถ is dropped.

F. Simple advice

> When **dâai** ได้ is placed after the main verb, it can be understood in terms of the action being possible *whatever the reason*. Whether it is translated in English as *can, being able to, being allowed to* or *permitted to* depends on the context.

In Thai, a statement can be complete without a subject if the subject is understood from the context. In English that is not usually possible.

Example:

> ทำ ได้
> *tham-dâai*
> do-can

Depending on the context, the English translations of this simple Thai sentence could include:

It is possible.

You can do it.

I am allowed to do it.

He is able to do it.

They can do it.

We are permitted to do it.

Everybody is able to do it.

It can be done. (passive voice)

etc.

In English, we usually need at least a subject, a verb and often an object in order to make a complete sentence. I addition, the tense must be correct.

In Thai, the correct meaning and the tense is usually understood from the context. Every word is in its basic form. Hence, verbs are not conjugated in Thai at all.

See more about how Thai uses tenses in the book II, Secrets 15–22.

Secret 4

dâai is very beautiful. She dresses well and always does her best whatever she is doing. **dâai** says: "Everybody should understand that behaving well and working hard are very important aspects of life."

ได้ สวย มาก – แต่ง ตัว เหมาะสม และ ทำ ทุก อย่าง – อย่าง ดี ที่ สุด เสมอ – ได้ บอก ว่า – ทุก คน ควร จะ เข้า ใจ ว่า การ ทำ ตัว และ การ ทำ งาน ให้ ดี เป็น ลักษณะ ที่ สำคัญ มาก ใน ชีวิต

dâai sŭuai mâak – tɛ̀ɛng-tuua mɔ̀sŏm lɛ́ tham thúk-yàang yàang-dii thîi-sùt sàmɛ̆ə – **dâai** bɔ̀ɔk-wâa – thúk-khon khuuan-tsà khâu-tsai wâa kaan tham-tuua lɛ́ kaan-tham-ngaan hâi-dii pen láksànà thîi sămkhan mâak nai tʃiiwít

dâai beautiful very – prepare-body proper and do every-kind kind-good that-most always – **dâai** say that – every-person should-will enter-heart that matter-do-body and matter-work give-good be quality that important very in life

dâai ได้ and adjectives

dâai ได้ can be placed before or after an adjective. When **dâai** ได้ is placed before an adjective, it turns an adjective into an *adverb*. When **dâai** ได้ is placed after an adjective, it is translated into English as *can, being able to* or *allowed to* do something in that way.

A. Sentences with dâai ได้ and adjectives

1 Beautifully – dâai-sǔuai ได้ สวย

Women walk *beautifully*.

ผู้หญิง เดิน ได้ สวย
phûu-yǐng dəən *dâai-sǔuai*
person-woman walk *can-beautiful*

1.1 Without dâai ได้

Women walk *beautifully*.

ผู้หญิง เดิน สวย
phûu-yǐng dəən *sǔuai*
person-woman walk *beautiful*

1.2 Able to, beautifully – sǔuai-dâai สวย ได้

Women *can* walk *beautifully*.

ผู้หญิง เดิน สวย ได้
phûu-yǐng dəən *sǔuai dâai*
person-woman walk *beautiful can*

2 Fluently – dâai-khlɔ̂ng ได้ คล่อง

Students speak English *fluently*.

นักเรียน พูด ภาษา อังกฤษ ได้ คล่อง
nákriian phûut phaasǎa anggrìt *dâai-khlɔ̂ng*
student speak language English *can-fluent*

2.1 Without dâai ได้

Students speak English *fluently*.

นัก เรียน พูด ภาษา อังกฤษ คล่อง
nákriian phûut phaasăa anggrìt *khlɔ̂ng*
student speak language English *skillful*

2.2 Able to, fluently – khlɔ̂ng-dâai คล่อง ได้

Students *are able to* speak English *fluently*.

นักเรียน พูด ภาษา อังกฤษ คล่อง ได้
nákriian phûut phaasăa anggrìt *khlɔ̂ng dâai*
student speak language English *fluent can*

3 Fast – dâai-reu ได้ เร็ว

He drives a car *fast*.

เขา ขับ รถ ได้ เร็ว
kháu khàp rót *dâai-reu*
he drive car *can-fast*

3.1 Without dâai ได้

He drives a car *fast*.

เขา ขับ รถ เร็ว
kháu khàp rót *reu*
he drive car *fast*

3.2 Able to, fast – reu-dâai เร็ว ได้

He *is able to* drive a car fast.

เขา ขับ รถ เร็ว ได้
kháu khàp rót *reu dâai*
he drive car *fast can*

B. Highlights

Here, we demonstrate what happens when **dâai** ได้ is placed after the main verb and before or after an adjective.

> When **dâai** ได้ is placed before an adjective, it turns an adjective into an *adverb*. There are also some elements of *"being able to"* do it that way. It can also be dropped; the translation into English is the same. However, in Thai, something is lost.
>
> When **dâai** ได้ is placed after an adjective, it is translated into English as *can, being able to* or *allowed to* do something in that way.

Consider the following:

A)   **dâai** ได้ before an adjective

> In the sentences 1–3 the emphasis is on the *doing it that way*. There are some elements of *being able to do* the action that way. It is commonly translated into English by using an *adverb*.

1   **phûu-yĭng dəən dâai-sŭuai**
ผู้หญิง เดิน ได้ สวย
Women walk beautifully.

2   **nákriian phûut phaasăa anggrìt dâai-khlɔ̂ng**
นักเรียน พูด ภาษา อังกฤษ ได้ คล่อง
Students speak English fluently.

Secret 4

> **3** **kháu khàp rót dâai-reu**
> เขา ขับ รถ ได้ เร็ว
> *He drives a car fast.*

The above structure (sentences 1–3) is commonly used when one sees or hears someone perform the action that way. The action is usually happening in the present time.

B) Dropping **dâai** ได้

> We can drop **dâai** ได้ before an adjective but the meaning is the same as in sentences 1–3. Only the colour of the sentence is different.

> **1.1** **phûu-yĭng dəən sŭuai**
> ผู้หญิง เดิน สวย
> *Women walk beautifully.*

> **2.1** **nákriian phûut phaasăa anggrìt khlɔ̂ng**
> นักเรียน พูด ภาษา อังกฤษ คล่อง
> *Students speak English fluently.*

> **3.1** **kháu khàp rót reu**
> เขา ขับ รถ เร็ว
> *He drives a car fast.*

Without **dâai** ได้ these sentences lack some elements of being able to perform action that way; however, the translation into English is the same as in the sentences 1–3.

C) **dâai** ได้ after an adjective

> Here, the emphasis is on the *ability* or *permission to* perform the action that way.

phûu-yǐng dəən sǔuai dâai
ผู้หญิง เดิน สวย ได้
Women can walk beautifully.

Depending on the context, the same can also be translated as *women are able* or *allowed to walk beautifully.*

nákriian phûut phaasǎa anggrìt khlɔ̂ng dâai
นักเรียน พูด ภาษา อังกฤษ คล่อง ได้
Students can speak English fluently.

Depending on the context, the same can also be translated as *students are able to speak English fluently* or *students are allowed to speak English fluently.* However, in real life the latter sounds a bit odd in any language.

kháu khàp rót reu dâai
เขา ขับ รถ เร็ว ได้
He can drive fast.

Depending on the context, the same can also be translated into English as *he is able* or *is allowed to drive fast* but he does not necessarily drive fast.

This structure is often used when one takes note that someone is able to perform the action that way. It does not mean that he/she necessarily does so.

C. Understanding dâai ได้

Generally, **dâai** ได้ can be understood as expressing a positive state of affairs, something that is possible.

Word order:

> 1. subject + verb + reu + **dâai** + adjective = *adverb, doing something in that way*
>
> kháu + khàp + **dâai** + **reu** = *He drives fast.*

when **dâai** ได้ is placed before an adjective in the sentence, it turns an adjective into an *adverb* and tells how or in what way someone is doing something.

> 2. subject + verb + adjective + **dâai** = *can, being able* or *being permitted to do something in that way*
>
> kháu + khàp + **reu** + **dâai** = *He can drive fast. He is able to drive fast. He is allowed to drive fast.*

When **dâai** ได้ is placed after an adjective in a sentence, then its semantic boundaries are defined by English words such as *can, being able to* or *being permitted to* perform the action *in that way*.

> 3. subject + verb + reu = *adverb, doing something in that way*
>
> kháu + khàp + reu = *He drives fast.*

We can drop **dâai** ได้ before an adjective, and the English translation is the same as in the first example. Only the colour of the statement is slightly different. Without **dâai** ได้, the sentence lacks some elements of *being able to* do it that way.

When **dâai** ได้ is placed after an adjective, it cannot be dropped without changing the meaning.

D. Conclusion

> Key: Place **dâai** ได้ before an adjective in a sentence in order to turn an adjective into an *adverb*. The meaning refers to *how* or *in what way* the action is being performed, physically or mentally. **dâai** ได้ can be also be dropped and the meaning remains the same or very similar.
>
> Place **dâai** ได้ after an adjective at the end of the sentence, and the meaning is clearly different. After an adjective the meaning is *being able to* or *permitted to* perform the action *in that way*, mentally or physically.

Sometimes, the difference in meaning is very subtle. We shall demonstrate this by giving more examples:

> **1** She wears clothes *beautifully*.
> เขา ใส่ เสื้อ ผ้า ได้ สวย
> kháu sài sûua-phâa *dâai-sŭuai*
> she wear shirt-cloth *can-beautiful*

Here, we have placed **dâai** ได้ before an adjective in a sentence. The adjective *beautiful* is turned into an adverb *beautifully*.

> **2** She wears clothes *beautifully*.
> เขา ใส่ เสื้อ ผ้า สวย
> kháu sài sûua-phâa *sŭuai*
> she wear shirt-cloth *beautiful*

dâai ได้ can also be dropped. Then the colour of the statement is slightly different. However, the translation into English is the same. When **dâai** ได้ is left out, the sentence lacks some elements of *being able to wear clothes beautifully*.

> **3** She wears *beautiful* clothes.
> เขา ใส่ เสื้อ ผ้า สวย
> kháu sài sûua-phâa *sǔuai*
> she wear shirt-cloth *beautiful*

In Thai, this sentence is written exactly the same as the sentence 2 but the translation into English is different. Depending on the context, this sentence could also be understood as *she wears clothes beautifully*.

In fact, here, the meaning is *she wears beautiful clothes now as we see it*. This type of statement usually refers only to one set of clothes or piece of cloth.

> **4** She wears *beautiful* clothes.
> เขา ใส่ เสื้อ ผ้า สวยๆ
> kháu sài sûua phâa *sǔuai-sǔuai*
> she wear shirt-cloth *beautiful-beautiful*

Here, we have doubled the adjective **sǔuai** สวย *beautiful*. This sentence is translated into English as *she wears beautiful clothes*. The sentence means that she behaves generally that way. It is her style. Compare this sentence with the sentences 2 and 3. This sentence can only be understood as *she wears beautiful clothes*.

> **5** She *can* wear *beautiful* clothes.
>
> เขา ใส่ เสื้อ ผ้า สวย ได้
> kháu sài sûua phâa *sǔuai dâai*
> she wear shirt-cloth *beautiful can*

Depending on the context, this sentence could also be translated into English as *she is permitted to* or *she is able to wear beautiful clothes* if she wants to. There must be a reason why. She may be rich or because of her social status etc.

In this structure, **dâai** ได้ cannot be dropped without changing the meaning. If we drop **dâai** ได้, then the translation into English would be the same as in the sentences 1, 2 or 3 *she wears clothes beautifully* or *she wears beautiful clothes*.

E. Language hints

A) Keep in mind that **dâai** ได้ brings something of herself into every statement, no matter what role she plays.

More examples:

> **1** dâai-reu ได้ เร็ว
>
> He drives a car fast.
>
> เขา ขับ รถ ได้ เร็ว
> kháu khàp rót *dâai-reu*
> he drive car *can-fast*

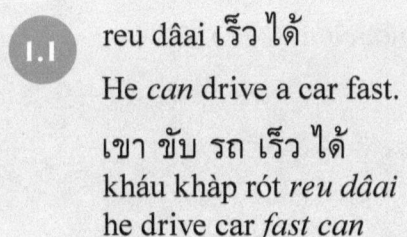

> **1.1** reu dâai เร็ว ได้
>
> He *can* drive a car fast.
>
> เขา ขับ รถ เร็ว ได้
> kháu khàp rót *reu dâai*
> he drive car *fast can*

Compare these sentences 1 and 1.1. In both sentences, we have included the helping verb **dâai** ได้ together with an adjective.

When **dâai** ได้ is placed before an adjective as in the sentence 1, it turns an adjective into an *adverb* and tells how, mentally or physically, someone is doing something.

However, in speaking, **dâai** ได้ is often dropped before an adjective to make the statement short.

When **dâai** ได้ is placed after an adjective as it can be translated into English as *can, to be able to* or *to be permitted to* do something that way.

In the sentence 1.1 **dâai** ได้ means that *he is able to drive fast*, but does not necessarily drive fast. When **dâai** ได้ is placed after an adjective, it cannot be dropped without changing the meaning.

Without **dâai** ได้ the above statement simply means he drives fast as in the sentence 1.

> **2** dâai ได้ with positive connotation
>
> She walks *beautifully*.
>
> เขา เดิน ได้ สวย
> kháu dəən *dâai-sŭuai*
> she walk *can-beautiful*

> **2.1** dâai ได้ with negative connotation
>
> He drives *badly*.
>
> เขา ขับ รถ ได้ แย่
> kháu khàp rót *dâai-yêɛ*
> he drive car *can-bad*

Compare these sentences 2 and 2.1. Both sentences are expressed by the English adverbs, *beautifully* and *badly* respectively.

We have pointed out several times before that **dâai** ได้ is usually understood by Thais as something positive. However, in some rare cases **dâai** ได้ can be placed before an adjective that has a negative connotation. They are very few. **dâai-yêɛ** ได้ แย่ *badly, terribly* is one of them.

> **3** dâai ได้ before a concrete noun
>
> We *got* a new car.
>
> เรา ได้ รถ คัน ใหม่
> rau *dâai* rót khan mài
> we *get* car-vehicle new

> **3.1** dâai ได้ before an abstract noun
>
> She *is* lucky.
>
> เขา ได้ ลาภ
> kháu *dâai* lâap
> she *get* luck

Compare these sentences 3 and 3.1. In both sentences **dâai** ได้ is placed before a noun.

In the sentence 3, **dâai** ได้ is placed before a concrete noun and is translated into English as *to get*.

In the sentence 3.1, **dâai** ได้ is placed before an abstract noun **lâap** ลาภ *luck;* that is translated into English as *to be lucky*. However, Thai people would think in terms of *to get luck, winning on lottery etc.*

---

4   dâai ได้ after an action verb

He *can* go out.

เขา ไป เที่ยว ได้
kháu pai thîiau *dâai*
he go tour *can*

4.1   dâai ได้ before an action verb

He *has gone* out.

เขา ได้ ไป เที่ยว
kháu *dâai* pai thîiau
he *get* go tour

Compare these sentences 4 and 4.1. In both sentences, **dâai** ได้ is used as a helping verb.

In the sentence 4, **dâai** ได้ is placed after the main verb **pai** ไป *to go*. The meaning is *he is able to, is allowed to* or *permitted to go*. He can go out whatever the reason.

In the sentence 4.1, **dâai** ได้ is placed before the main verb **pai** ไป *to go;* that is translated into English as *he has gone out*. The past time is understood from the context. Thai people usually think in terms of *"getting"* the action in question. We shall review **dâai** ได้ before the action verb in Secret 5.

B) There are several other words that can be put before adjectives in order to turn them into adverbs. The most common are:

yàang อย่าง, **bὲεp** แบบ and **hâi** ให้. These words are sometimes interchangeable, but often have a different colour in the sentence and also a different meaning.

> **1** Safely – yàang-plɔ̀ɔt-phai อย่าง ปลอดภัย
>
> We arrived here *safely*.
>
> เรา มา ถึง ที่ นี่ อย่าง ปลอดภัย
> rau maa thǔng thîi-nîi *yàang plɔ̀ɔt-phai*
> we come reach place this *as-safe*

yàang plɔ̀ɔt-phai อย่าง ปลอดภัย *safely*

One way to turn an adjective into an adverb is to use **yàang** อย่าง *way, sort*. The meaning is a bit different when compared to **dâai** ได้. **yàang** อย่าง + adjective describes the fact *how* or *in what way* the action is happening.

> **2** Properly – yàang-mɔ̀sǒm อย่าง เหมาะ สม
>
> He did it *properly*.
>
> เขา ทำ มัน อย่าง เหมาะ สม
> kháu tham man *yàang-mɔ̀sǒm*
> he do it *as-proper*

yàang-mɔ̀sǒm อย่าง เหมาะ สม *properly*

This structure is not a "command" but rather tells *in what way* one is doing something.

yàang อย่าง before an adjective may be dropped and the meaning is the same. Only the colour of the statement is different.

> **3** Seriously – yàang-tsing-tsang อย่าง จริง จัง
>
> *Seriously*, I need to talk with him.
>
> ฉัน ต้อง คุย กับ เขา อย่าง จริง จัง
> ṭǎn tôŋ khui gàp kháu *yàang-tsing-tsang*
> I need talk with he *as-true-real*

yàang-tsing-tsang อย่าง จริง จัง *seriously*

This structure is not a command but rather tells *in what way* one is doing something.

yàang อย่าง before an adjective may be dropped and the meaning is the same. Only the colour of the statement is different.

> **4** Contentedly – bɛ̀ɛp-sàbaai-sàbaai แบบ สบายๆ
>
> He works *contentedly*.
>
> เขา ทำ งาน แบบ สบายๆ
> kháu tham-ngaan *bɛ̀ɛp-sàbaai-sàbaai*
> he do-work *style-fine-fine*

bɛ̀ɛp sàbaai-sàbaai แบบ สบายๆ *contentedly*

bɛ̀ɛp แบบ + adjective describes *in what style* an action is happening. This structure is not a command but rather tells *in what style* he is doing something.

bɛ̀ɛp แบบ before an adjective may be dropped and the meaning remains the same. Only the colour of the statement is different.

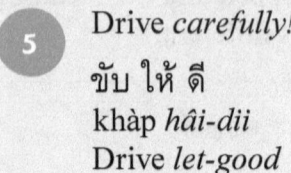

5 Drive *carefully!*
ขับ ให้ ดี
khàp *hâi-dii*
Drive *let-good*

hâi-dii ให้ ดี *carefully*

hâi ให้ before the adjective emphasizes the idea of how one should behave, here *driving well, carefully.*

This structure is a command!

hâi ให้ before an adjective may be dropped and the meaning remains the same. Only the colour of the statement is different. In that case, the adjective is often doubled and the sentence becomes **khàp dii-dii** ขับ ดีๆ *drive carefully.*

If you want to learn more about how to use the verb **hâi** ให้ in sentences, an excellent review of it can be found in the book *Learning Thai with hâi* ให้ *– 22 Secrets of Learning Thai.*

c) In Thai, adjectives can perform the role of an *adverb* and even the role of a *verb* in a sentence.

When speaking, Thais like to make everything simple and short. The correct meaning is often understood from the context and the way the statement is said. Therefore, **dâai** ได้ can be dropped, and an adjective is used alone to perform different grammatical meanings.

Examples:

She *is a good* person.
เขา เป็น คน ดี
kháu *pen* khon *dii*
she *be* person *good*

dii ดี *good* is used here as an adjective. When we use the verb **pen** เป็น *to be*, then it must be followed by a noun. Here, the classifier, **khon** คน *person,* is used.

She *is a good* person.
เขา ดี
kháu *dii*
she *good*

pen เป็น *to be* and **khon** คน *person* may be dropped.

Here, the adjective **dii** ดี *good* also plays the role of the verb *to be*.

This is a simple way to say the same as in the previous sentence 1.

Warning:

It is not correct to say:
เขา เป็น ดี
kháu pen *dii*
she be *good*

pen เป็น *to be* is a special verb in the sense that it must be followed by a noun.

Here, it is followed by an adjective **dii** ดี *good*. Therefore, this statement is grammatically wrong. It can be understood but it sounds odd to Thais. See the sentence 1.

She works *well*.

เขา ทำ งาน ดี
kháu tham-ngaan *dii*
she do work *good*

Here, the adjective **dii** ดี *good* plays the role of the adverb *well, efficiently*.

Depending on the context, **dii** ดี means in English *good, is good, well, efficiently*.

Since everything in Thai is in its basic form, there is no need to consider whether an adjective is an adjective, an adverb or a verb.

Generally, Thai people do not think in terms of adjectives playing different roles. But perhaps, we westerners will understand the Thai language more easily if we make that distinction. After all, we are trying to understand Thai with the help of the English language.

F. Simple advice

Since in this book we are looking at the world through the eyes of **dâai** ได้, we are trying to use it as much as possible in different types of example sentences.

Usually, ordinary Thai people are only intuitively aware of the meaning of **dâai** ได้ when it is used in different positions in a sentence. They cannot usually, therefore, give you an exact translation or explanation in English. Sometimes, it is not possible since English uses a different kind of syntax.

Even if you were a professional translator, you would need to know the context in order to give an accurate translation. Often, there could be several different possibilities for translation. To translate from one language to another is an art.

Often, Thais don't quite understand why "westerners" want to know the exact meaning of Thai words like **dâai** ได้. For Thai people, words are only an indication of something, and if the sentence sounds good, then there is not usually any problem. You can always ask for more information if needed.

> A sentence sounds good in Thai, if you are aware of the context, are able to choose simple common words and make the word order correct. Thais do have some difficulty in understanding you if you choose to use uncommon words that are not normally used in the relevant situation, no matter how correct you are grammatically. English is more easily understood even if you speak it your own way.

Secret 5

dâai is a person, who can change her place and the meaning of herself very easily. **dâai** says: "I can transform myself easily. We must understand that life changes all the time, and we should learn how to adjust ourselves."

ได้ เป็น คน ที่ เปลี่ยน ตำแหน่ง และ ความ หมาย ของ ตัวเอง ได้ ง่ายๆ – ได้ บอก ว่า – ฉัน พลิก แพลง ได้ ง่ายๆ – เรา ต้อง เข้า ใจ ว่า ชีวิต เปลี่ยน แปลง ตลอด เวลา และ เรา ต้อง รู้ ว่า จะ ปรับ ตัว ยัง ไง

dâai pen khon thîi plìian tam-nèɛng lé khwaam-măai khɔ̌ɔng tuua-eeng dâai ngâai-ngâai – **dâai** bɔ̀ɔk-wâa – tʃán phlík-phlɛɛng dâai ngâai-ngâai – rau tôŋ khâu-tsai wâa tʃiiwít plìian-phlɛɛng tàlɔ̀ɔt weelaa – rau tôŋ rúu wâa tsà pràp-tuua yang-ngai

dâai be person that change position and subject-meaning of body-self can easy-easy – **dâai** say that – I turn-twist can easy-easy – we must enter-heart that life changes all-time and we should-will adjust body-self for good increase

dâai ได้ as a helping verb before the main verb

dâai ได้ can be placed before the main verb in order to place emphasis on "getting" the action. In some cases, it can be translated into English as *to have an opportunity to* perform the action in question.

A. Sentences with dâai ได้ before the main verb

1 Ongoing activity, does work – dâai tham-ngaan
ได้ ทำ งาน

Now, he *does work* at Toyota.

ตอน นี้ เขา ได้ ทำ งาน ที่ บริษัท โตโยต้า
tɔɔn-níi kháu *dâai tham-ngaan* thîi bɔɔrísàt tooyootâa
at-this he *get do-work* at company Toyota

1.1 Without dâai ได้

Now, he *works* at Toyota.

ตอนนี้ เขา ทำ งาน ที่ บริษัท โตโยต้า
tɔɔn-níi kháu *tham-ngaan* thîi bɔɔrísàt tooyootâa
At-this he *do-work* at company Toyota

2 A completed action, did buy, have bought
– dâai súu... maa-lɛ́ɛu ได้ ซื้อ... มา แล้ว

I already *did* buy a pizza.

ฉัน ได้ ซื้อ พิซซ่า มา แล้ว
tʃán *dâai súu* phítsâa maa lɛ́ɛu
I *get-buy* pizza come already

2.1 Without dâai ได้

I *have* already *bought* a pizza.

ฉัน ซื้อ พิซซ่า มา แล้ว
tʃán *súu* phítsâa maa lɛ́ɛu
I *buy* pizza come already

3 A future with an if clause – If I get an opportunity to meet... thâa dâai tɕəə... ถ้า ได้ เจอ...

If I *get an opportunity to meet* a new woman who is kind, I'll stop drinking.

ถ้า ได้ เจอ ผู้หญิง คน ใหม่ – ที่ ใจ ดี – ผม จะ หยุด กิน เหล้า

thâa *dâai-tɕəə* phûu-yǐng khon mài – thîi tɕai-dii – phǒm tɕà yùt kin lâu

if *get-meet* person-women person new – that heart-good – I will stop eat alcohol

3.1 Without dâai ได้

If I *meet* a new women who is kind, I'll stop drinking.

ถ้า เจอ ผู้หญิง คน ใหม่ – ที่ ใจ ดี – ผม จะ หยุด กิน เหล้า

thâa *tɕəə* phûu-yǐng khon mài thîi tɕai-dii – phǒm tɕà yùt kin lâu

If *meet* person-women person new – that heart-good – I will stop eat alcohol

4 A question, did you get an opportunity to go or not? – khun dâai pai... lɛ́ɛu rǔɯ-yang คุณ ได้ ไป... แล้ว หรือ ยัง

Did you already *get an opportunity to go* to Japan or not?

คุณ ได้ ไป ญี่ปุ่น แล้ว หรือ ยัง

khun *dâai pai* yîipùn lɛ́ɛu rǔɯ-yang

you *get go* Japan already or-not

4.1 Without dâai

Did you already *go* to Japan or not?

คุณ ไป ญี่ปุ่น แล้ว หรือ ยัง
khun *pai* yîipùn lɛ́ɛu rǔɯ-yang
you *go* Japan already or-not

5 A negative statement, did not get an opportunity mâi-dâai ไม่ ได้

I *didn't get an opportunity to go* to Japan.

ฉัน ไม่ ได้ ไป ญี่ปุ่น
tʃán *mâi-dâai* pai yîipùn
I *no-get* go Japan

5.1 Without dâai

I *am not going*/I *won't go* to Japan.

ฉัน ไม่ ไป ญี่ปุ่น
tʃán *mâi* pai
I *no* go Japan

B. Highlights

Here, we have placed **dâai** ได้ before the main verb. In this context, **dâai** ได้ is often used in connection with the past. However, **dâai** ได้ may also be used in connection with present or future time activities when placed before the main verb. The feeling is one of *"getting it"*.

The Thai way to understand **dâai** ได้ before the action verb is *to obtain* or *to get* the action in question. Often, there is no direct way to translate this into English. Sometimes, it could be translated into English as *to get an opportunity* or a *chance to* do something.

The correct meaning of **dâai** ได้ before the action verb is *"getting"* the action in question, *an opportunity has arisen* and *also been taken*.

We can drop **dâai** ได้ but then the meaning loses something. Without **dâai** ได้ it becomes a blunt statement. The colour of the statement is different. There isn't any feeling of *"getting"* the action or *getting an opportunity* or *a chance to* do the action in question.

Consider the following:

1. Present

tɔɔn-níi kháu (dâai) tham-ngaan thîi bɔɔrísàt tooyootâa
ตอน นี้ เขา (ได้) ทำ งาน ที่ บริษัท โตโยต้า
Now, he does work at Toyota.

When we place **dâai** ได้ before the action verb **tham-ngaan** ทำ งาน as in the sentence 1, there is a clear reference to the fact that he has *obtained* the action to work at Toyota. He *did* take the opportunity to work. This means that the opportunity had opened up to him to work at Toyota, and he has taken it. Now, he *does* work at Toyota.

Now, he "gets" to work at Toyota. This is perhaps the most correct translation of the above sentence. The problem with this translation is that no English teacher would approve it because it is considered to be broken English or casual slang.

dropping **dâai** ได้
In English, most people would express both sentences 1 and 1.1 simply as *now, he works at Toyota.*

However, the sentence without **dâai** ได้ is a blunt statement (he works) without any reference to *"getting" to* or *getting an opportunity to* work at Toyota.

2. Past

tʃán (dâai) súu phítsâa maa lέεu
ฉัน (ได้) ซื้อ พิซซ่า มา แล้ว
I already did buy a pizza.

When we place **dâai** ได้ before the action verb **súu** ซื้อ *to buy* as in the sentence 2, there is a clear reference to the fact that she has a pizza now. She *did* take the opportunity to buy a pizza.

maa-lέεu มา แล้ว *come-already* at the end of the sentence means that the pizza is with her now. The action has been completed and she is probably enjoying eating it now.

I already "got" to buy a pizza. See the explanation in the sentence 1 above.

dropping **dâai** ได้
In English, most people would express both sentences 2 and 2.1 simply as *I have already bought a pizza.*

However, the sentence without **dâai** ได้ is a blunt statement; there is not any reference to *"getting" to* or *getting an opportunity to* buy a pizza.

3. Future

**thâa (dâai) tsəə phûu-yĭng khon mài thîi tsai-dii
– phŏm tsà yùt kin lâu**
ถ้า (ได้) เจอ ผู้หญิง คน ใหม่ – ที่ ใจ ดี – ผม จะ หยุด กิน เหล้า
If I get an opportunity to meet a new woman who is kind, I'll stop drinking.

In the above sentence 3, the meaning is that if the *opportunity* to meet *opens up, then* he will...

In English, we use *the present simple tense* here (If I get...). The future is understood from the *if clause*.

If I get to meet a new woman who is kind, I'll stop drinking.

We can drop **dâai** ได้ but then the sentence is a blunt statement which doesn't express the fact of *"getting"*, *having a chance* or getting an *opportunity to meet*.

4. Questions

khun (dâai) pai yîipùn lɛ́ɛu rŭu-yang
คุณ (ได้) ไป ญี่ปุ่น แล้ว หรือ ยัง
Did you already get an opportunity to go to Japan or not?

When we state a question as in the sentence 4, **dâai** ได้ can be translated into English as *to get an opportunity to go*.

Did you already get to go to Japan or not? See also the explanation in the sentence 1, page 87.

We can drop **dâai** ได้, but then the sentence is a blunt statement which doesn't express the fact of *"getting"*, *having a chance* or an *opportunity to* go. It is then translated into English as *did you already go to Japan or not?*

5. Negative statements

 tʃán mâi-dâai pai
ฉัน ไม่ ได้ ไป
I *didn't get an opportunity* to go.

In the negative past time phrase as in the sentence 5, **dâai** ได้ is usually included and cannot be dropped. **mâi-dâai** ไม่ ได้, before the main verb, is often understood as a *past simple tense*, *did not get an opportunity to*.

 If we drop **dâai** ได้ in the negative phrase, as in the sentence, the tenses changes from the negative past to the negative future, *I won't go* or *I am not going.*

C. Understanding dâai ได้

Generally, **dâai** ได้ can be understood as expressing a positive state of affairs, something that is possible.

The feeling is *"getting"* it.

dâai ได้ can be used grammatically in different ways. For Thai people, **dâai** ได้ is one word, however. They use it very intuitively and do not usually think in terms of its different meanings.

In Secret 3, we have placed **dâai** ได้ after the action verb. The meaning is *can, to be able* or *being permitted to do something.*

> In this Secret, we have placed **dâai** ได้ before the action verb. We need to change our thinking from *can* to *get*.
>
> We are making here some extra effort to explain the meaning of **dâai** ได้ when it is placed before the action verb because the direct translation into English is not always readily available.

Many books don't give any translation for the helping verb **dâai** ได้ when it is placed before the action verb. Some books point out that this structure is not very common in Thai. However, Thai people use **dâai** ได้ before the action verb a lot. Therefore, we try to do our best in order to give you a satisfactory explanation and translation of **dâai** ได้.

Word order:

> subject + **dâai** + verb + lɛ́ɛu = *"getting" the action in question in the past*
>
> kháu + **dâai** + pai + Bangkok + lɛ́ɛu = depending on the context and style, we could give here several different translations into English as follows:

He already did go to Bangkok.

He already went to Bangkok.

He has already gone to Bangkok.

He already had a chance or *an opportunity to go to Bangkok etc.*

The Thai meaning of **dâai** ได้ before the action verb is *"getting"* the action in question, *the opportunity arose and the action was taken*. The tense can refer to present, past and future. **lɛ́ɛu** แล้ว *already* makes clear here that the action is refering to the past.

> If you need to translate **dâai** ได้ into English when placed before the action verb, then things become somewhat more complicated. There are several different possibilities depending on the context. In some cases, we may run into unnatural usage of English.

Consider the following explanations when **dâai** ได้ is placed before the main verb.

1. Ongoing action – *do, does, to be lucky, "sitting pretty"*

   > When **dâai** ได้ refers to the present *ongoing* activities, there isn't a single word that can express this simple fact in English. The Thai people understand this as *"getting" the action* in question.

   In English, for present time actions, the verb *to do,* is often placed before the base form of another verb to emphasize the importance of the action. This is one of the ways to translate **dâai** ได้ when it is placed before the action verb. However, this translation may sound unnatural in English and is not always accurate.

   In English, there is one nice idiom that may help you to understand the meaning of **dâai** ได้ when placed before the action verb, *"sitting pretty"*. That means that the *opportunity has been taken* and one is enjoying the situation. In Thai, we can express the same with **dâai** ได้ before the action verb. The desired action has been taken and now the person *feels happy.*

2. Completed action in the past

   Similarly, for past time actions the English verb *to do (did)* is often placed before the base form of another verb to emphasize the importance of an action that happened in the past.

The English usage of *did* before another verb often refers to an earlier statement that requires confirmation. Example: *Did* you go... ? Yes, I *did* go...

3. **mii ookàat** มี โอกาส *to get* or *have an opportunity*

    Often in Thai, we could used the phrase **mii ookàat** มี โอกาส *to have an opportunity to* instead of **dâai** ได้ before the action verb. However, the colour of the statement is different.

    > Sometimes, the English phrase *to have an opportunity to* or *to get an opportunity to* can also be given as a translation. This is particularly true with those cases when *opportunity* was there but was *not taken* or has *not yet been taken*.

    When asking questions, stating a fact about a negative statement in the past or speaking about future possibilities, the word *opportunity* could be given as a translation.

4. Get to?

    Can we translate **dâai** ได้ before the action verb as *"get to"*, (*"get to go"* etc.)? The answer is yes! However, this kind of English will not be approved by English language teachers or by those who like to maintain the correct usage of British English.

    The problem is that this kind of expression is not considered to be correct usage of the English word *to get* that has many different meanings. Also, using *"get to"* would not be very appropriate since it is considered to be a kind of *casual slang*. It doesn't stand up to this beautiful ancient Thai word **dâai** ได้.

    > If we need to choose only one word, the irony is that *"get to"* is perhaps the best English estimation of the word **dâai** ได้ when it is placed before the action verb. So, if your emphasis is only on understanding and not on the translation, then *"get to"* is fine.

5. **dâai** ได้ before the main verb together with other words

dâai ได้ is seldom used *alone* before the main verb without additional indicators that tell whether the action happened in the past, is happening in the present or will be happening in the future. This is because of the possibility of being misunderstood. See the sentences 1.1–5.2 on the previous pages and the following Language hints section E.

Here are some common words used when **dâai** ได้ is placed before the action verb.

A) **tɔɔn-níi** ตอน นี้ *now*

When **dâai** ได้ before the action verb is used in the present time sentence, it is usually used together with present time words like **tɔɔn-níi** ตอน นี้ *now*.

B) **lɛ́ɛu** แล้ว *already* or **maa-lɛ́ɛu** มา แล้ว *come already*

When **dâai** ได้ is used in the past time sentence, it is often used together with **lɛ́ɛu** แล้ว *already* or with **maa-lɛ́ɛu** มา แล้ว *come already*.

Also, past time words like **mûua-waan** เมื่อวาน *yesterday* can be used to give more information about the action.

C) **thâa-dâai** ถ้า ได้ *if* and **tsà** จะ *will*

When **dâai** ได้ is used in the *future time sentence*, it is often used together with the *if clause* **thâa-dâai** ถ้า ได้. The word *if* refers usually to the future. Also, future time words like **phrûng-níi** พรุ่งนี้ *tomorrow* or the future tense marker **tsà** จะ *will* can be used to express the anticipated future actions.

dâai ได้ can always be dropped, but then the colour of the statement is different. It would be a blunt statement without **dâai** ได้. There would not be any reference to *"getting", having an opportunity* or a *chance to* perform the action in question.

D) **mâi-dâai** ไม่ ได้ before the main verb

The negative past time sentences with **mâi-dâai** ไม่ ได้ express meanings like *did not,* or *did not get an opportunity to.*

In the negative past time sentences, **dâai** ได้ cannot usually be dropped.

mâi-dâai ไม่ ได้, when placed before the action verb, is usually understood as a past time action.

D. Conclusion

> Key: To understand **dâai** ได้ before the action verb is very easy. Think as Thai people do! In Thai, we can actually *get actions* as well as *things*. There seems not to be any difference in understanding whether we *"get to go"* or *"get an apple"* in Thai.

1. Place **dâai** ได้ before a main verb when you would like to emphasize the act of *"getting"* or *"obtaining"* to do something. **dâai** ได้ can be placed before action verbs to express *present, past* and *future time* activities.

2. When **dâai** ได้ is placed before an action verb, it is not always very easy to translate the exact meaning into English. However, for Thai people, it means *to get* the action in question that has become possible. It is simple like that. It is better not to get stuck with the English translation.

3. Simply, **dâai** ได้ can be placed before *verbs* and also before *nouns*. The English verb *to get,* which has a number of different usages, is not usually placed before verbs. Yet, in very informal speaking style *get to do (if I get to go)* is used by some people, particularly in America.

4. Here, we have given somewhat sophisticated explanations of **dâai** ได้ before action verbs. This is because the English language uses a different kind of syntax and quite complicated structure of tenses. When we are trying to understand what role **dâai** ได้ plays when it is placed before the action verb, the key is to keep it simple. **dâai** ได้ gives a statement certain colour that is intuitively understood by Thai people as *"getting" something.*

5. **dâai** ได้, before the action verb, can be used in the sentences which denote the present, past or future tenses. For deeper analyses of how the present, past and future is expressed in Thai, see the Book II, Learning Thai Tenses with **dâai** ได้, Secrets 15–22.

6. One more observation about **dâai** ได้, before an action verb, is that without it life would be a bit boring. When **dâai** ได้ is left out, something is lost for sure. In this sense, Thai is sometimes more expressive than English.

E. Language hints

Even though **dâai** ได้ before the main verb is often used in connection with past time activities, it would be wrong to conclude that **dâai** ได้ is a past tense marker.

If there isn't any other indicator that suggests differently, in the negative past time sentences, **mâi-dâai** ไม่ได้ expresses usually the past tense.

In positive past time sentences, when **dâai** ได้ is placed before the action verb, another word such as **lɛ́ɛu** แล้ว *already* is often used to make the past tense clear.

We shall review the Thai tenses later in the Book II, Secrets 15–22. So, just for now, note that if we place **dâai** ได้ alone before an action verb, there would be several ways to understand the statement unless the context is known.

Consider the following:

> **1** Past time with **dâai** ได้ and **lɛ́ɛu** แล้ว
>
> He *already did* go to Ko Samui.
>
> เขา ได้ ไป เกาะ สมุย แล้ว
> kháu *dâai* pai kɔ̀-sàmŭi *lɛ́ɛu*
> he *get* go Ko Samui *already*

Often when **dâai** ได้ is used in connection with the past, it is used with another word such as **lɛ́ɛu** แล้ว *already*. This is a past time sentence with **dâai** ได้ that carries some elements of *"getting"* to go.

> **2** Dropping dâai ได้
>
> He *already* went to Ko Samui.
>
> เขา ไป เกาะ สมุย แล้ว
> kháu pai kɔ̀-sàmŭi *lɛ́ɛu*
> he go Ko Samui *already*

dâai ได้ can also be dropped, and the statement still expresses past time. **lɛ́ɛu** แล้ว is enough to express the past tense here, but the colour of the statement changes to become more of a blunt statement. There is not any reference to *"getting" to go* or *getting an opportunity to go*.

3 Using dâai ได้ alone

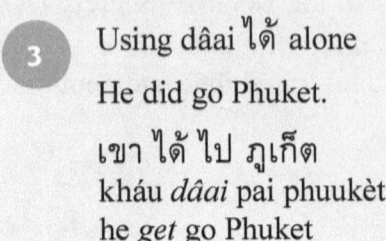

He did go Phuket.

เขา ได้ ไป ภูเก็ต
kháu *dâai* pai phuukèt
he *get* go Phuket

Here, **dâai** ได้ is placed *alone* before the action verb, and the word **lɛ́ɛu** แล้ว *already* is dropped. The meaning, in terms of whether he has already gone, is not very clear.

There is the certainty of something happening with him going to Phuket.

In the absence of time words, the tense in Thai is usually understood from the context. Hence, there could be several ways to translate this statement into English unless the context is known:

a) *He did go to Phuket.* He has taken the opportunity and is in Phuket now.

b) *He has gone to Phuket.* He is in Phuket now.

c) *He went to Phuket.* The statement refers to a certain time like yesterday.

d) *He has been to Phuket.* He is already back from Phuket.

e) *He has an opportunity to go to Phuket.* He did not yet go to Phuket, but can go.

4 Did not go – mâi-dâai pai ไม่ ได้ ไป

He *didn't* go to Phuket.

เขา ไม่ ได้ ไป ภูเก็ต
kháu *mâi-dâai* pai phuukèt
he *no-get* go Phuket

mâi-dâai ไม่ ได้ before the action verb usually expresses a *past tense*.

Depending on the context this sentence could also be translated into English as *he didn't get an opportunity to go to Phuket*.

In the negative past time sentences, **dâai** ได้ is usually included and cannot be dropped.

F. Simple advice

dâai ได้ is quite a sophisticated word, and Thai people use it intuitively in many different ways to express themselves. One thing to keep in mind is that, whenever you see **dâai** ได้ in the sentence, she brings something of herself into the meaning. She brings some special feeling into the statement.

In this Secret, we have given a lot of complicated explanations of **dâai** ได้ when it is placed before the action verb. Yet, we could have just said that it means *get to* in English. The truth of the matter is that when you ask Thai or foreign people, including language teachers, how **dâai** ได้ is translated into English when placed before an action verb, you will get many different kinds of answers. That does not mean that they are not able to use **dâai** ได้ correctly. It only means that the translation into English is not always readily available.

> As far as the Thai language is concerned, using **dâai** ได้ before the action verb is very simple. Think like a Thai! Then you would be *"getting"* all types of actions in the same way as you would be *"getting"* things like *apples, computers, houses* etc.

Generally, if we need to give a simple translation of the verb **dâai** ได้ in English, it should be the two verbs *to get* and *can*. Before the action verb, the meaning is *to get* and after the action verb the meaning is *can, being able to* or *being permitted to.*

Secret 6

dâai ได้ is a person who always likes to help other people. **dâai** ได้ says: "Always do your best."

ได้ เป็น คน ที่ ชอบ ช่วย คน อื่น ตลอด เวลา – ได้ บอก ว่า – จง ทำ ทุก อย่าง ให้ ดี ที่ สุด เสมอ

dâai pen khon thîi tʃɔ́ɔp tʃûuai khon ɯ̀ɯn tàlɔ̀ɔt-wee-laa – **dâai** bɔ̀ɔk-wâa – tsong tham thúk yàang hâi dii thîi-sùt sàmɤ̌ɤ

dâai be person that like help person other entire-time – **dâai** say that – must do every kind let good that-most always

dâai ได้ and some special verbs

dâai ได้ is often used together with some special verbs to form new meanings.

Good examples are **dâai-yin** ได้ ยิน *to hear*, **dâai-rúu** ได้ รู้ *to discover*, and **dâai-ráp** ได้ รับ *to receive* or *to be received*.

A. Sentences with dâai ได้ and special verbs

1 To hear – dâai-yin ได้ ยิน

I *heard* a loud noise coming from the neighbour's house.

ฉัน ได้ ยิน เสียง ดัง มา จาก ข้าง บ้าน
tʃǎn *dâai-yin* sǐiang dang maa tsàak khâang-bâan
I *get-hear* sound loud come from next-house

1.1 To listen – fang ฟัง

I *listened* to the music coming from the neighbour's house.

ฉัน ได้ ฟัง เพลง ที่ มา จาก ข้าง บ้าน
tʃǎn *dâai fang* pleng thîi maa tsàak khâang-bâan
I *get listen* music that come from next-house

2 To discover – dâai-rúu ได้ รู้

I *discovered* an excellent new way to study.

ฉัน ได้ รู้ วิธี ใหม่ ที่ จะ ทำ ให้ เรียน เก่ง
tʃǎn *dâai-rúu* wíthii mài thîi tsà tham hâi riian kèng
I *get-know* way new that will do make study excellent

2.1 To find, to meet – tsəə เจอ

I *found* an excellent new way to study.

ฉัน ได้ เจอ วิธี ใหม่ ที่ จะ ทำ ให้ เรียน เก่ง
tʃǎn *dâai tsəə* wíthii mài thîi tsà tham-hâi riian kèng
I *get meet* way new that will do make study excellent

2.2 To find out, to discover – khón-phóp ค้น พบ

I *found* an excellent new way to study.

ฉัน ได้ ค้น พบ วิธี ใหม่ ที่ จะ ทำ ให้ เรียน เก่ง
tʃán *dâai khón-phóp* wíthii mài thîi tsà tham-hâi riian kèng
I *get search-meet* way new that will do make study excellent

3 To be invited – dâai-ráp-tʃɔɔn ได้ รับ เชิญ

I *was invited* by him to go to study.

ฉัน ได้ รับ เชิญ จาก เขา ให้ ไป เรียน
tʃán *dâai-ráp-tʃɔɔn* tsàak kháu hâi pai riian
I *get-receive-invite* from he give go study

3.1 To invite – tʃɔɔn เชิญ

He *invited* me to go to study.

เขา ได้ เชิญ ฉัน ไป เรียน
kháu *dâai tʃɔɔn* tʃán pai riian
he *get invite* I go study

B. Highlights

dâai ได้ can be placed before some special verbs in a similar manner to that we already studied in Secret 5.

However, the meaning and the function of the verb **dâai** ได้ is somewhat different in this Secret.

Consider the following:

> **1 tʃán dâai-yin sĭiang dang maa tsàak khâang-bân**
> ฉัน ได้ ยิน เสียง ดัง มา จาก ข้าง บ้าน
> *I heard a loud noise coming from the neighbour's house.*

dâai-yin ได้ ยิน means *to hear*. **dâai-yin** ได้ ยิน is a special verb combination in the sense that these two verbs **dâai** ได้ and **yin** ยิน cannot be separated. They must go together. **yin** ยิน means *to hear* and is not usually used alone. So, literally the Thai way to express the verb *to hear* is *get-hear*.

> **1.1 tʃán (dâai) fang pleng thîi maa tsàak khâang-bân**
> ฉัน (ได้) ฟัง เพลง ที่ มา จาก ข้าง บ้าน
> *I listened to the music coming from the neighbour's house.*

dâai fang ได้ ฟัง is an ordinary verb contruction in the sense that here **dâai** ได้ plays the role of a helping verb only, in the same way we learned in the previous Secret 5.

fang ฟัง *to listen* can be used alone without **dâai** ได้, and the translation into English does not change. Then, the meaning is just *to listen* and *not "getting" to listen*.

> **2 tʃán dâai-rúu wíthii mài thîi tsà tham hâi riian kèng**
> ฉัน ได้ รู้ วิธี ใหม่ ที่ จะ ทำ ให้ เรียน เก่ง
> *I discovered an excellent new way to study.*

dâai-rúu ได้ รู้ means *to find, to discover*. **dâai-rúu** ได้ รู้ is a kind of a special verb combination in the sense that the translation of the verb **rúu** รู้ *to know* changes to *to discover* in English. The Thai way to think about **dâai-rúu** ได้ รู้ is, however, *"getting" to know*.

tʃán (dâai) tsəə wíthii mài thîi tsà tham-hâi riian kèng
ฉัน (ได้) เจอ วิธี ใหม่ ที่ จะ ทำ ให้ เรียน เก่ง
I found an excellent new way to study.

dâai tsəə ได้ เจอ is an ordinary verb contruction in the sense that here **dâai** ได้ plays the role of a helping verb only in the same way we learned in the previous Secret. The verb **tsəə** เจอ *to find* can be used alone without **dâai** ได้, and the translation into English is the same. Then, the meaning is just *to find* and not *"getting" to find*.

The verb **tsəə** เจอ is commonly used in connection with *to meet* someone. It can also be used in the sense of *to find, to discover* something.

 tʃán (dâai) khón-phóp wíthii mài thîi tsà tham-hâi riian kèng
ฉัน ได้ ค้น พบ วิธี ใหม่ ที่ จะ ทำ ให้ เรียน เก่ง
I found an excellent new way to study.

This is an alternative way to express the meaning of the verb *to discover*. **khón** ค้น alone means *to search* and **phóp** พบ alone means *to find, to meet, to discover*. **khón-phóp** ค้น พบ is a bit more formal in style than **dâai-rúu** ได้ รู้ or **tsəə** เจอ *to find out, to discover*.

The verb combination **dâai khón-phóp** ได้ ค้น พบ is an ordinary verb combination in the sense that here **dâai** ได้ plays the role of a helping verb only. **khón-phóp** ค้น พบ can be used alone without **dâai** ได้, and the translation into English does not change.

 tʃán dâai-ráp-tʃəən tsàak kháu hâi pai riian
ฉัน ได้ รับ เชิญ จาก เขา ให้ ไป เรียน
I was invited by him to go to study.

dâai-ráp-tʃɔɔn ได้ รับ เชิญ is a special verb combination in the sense that it is often translated into English as a passive voice.

However, Thai people do not usually think of this structure as a passive voice but rather as an active voice, *I received an invitation from him to go to study.*

kháu (dâai) tʃɔɔn tʃán pai riian
เขา (ได้) เชิญ ฉัน ไป เรียน
He invited me to go to study.

In this sentence, we have dropped the verb **ráp** รับ, and the meaning is different. The grammatical English form has changed from *I was invited by him to go to study* to *he invited me to go to study.*

dâai tʃɔɔn ได้ เชิญ is an ordinary verb combination in the sense that the verb **tʃɔɔn** เชิญ *to invite* can be used alone without **dâai** ได้, and is usually translated into English as an active voice.

C. Understanding dâai ได้

Generally, **dâai** ได้ can be understood as expressing a positive state of affairs, something that is possible.

dâai ได้ can be used with some special verbs to form new meanings.

These verbs are rather more like compound verbs. They cannot be separated without changing the meaning. They are commonly used for mental activities. Here are some common examples:

dâai-yin	ได้ ยิน	*to hear*
dâai-rúu	ได้ รู้	*to discover*
dâai-khít	ได้ คิด	*to realise, to understand*
dâai-ráp	ได้ รับ	*as a passive voice*

Word order:

> 1. Subject + **dâai** + a special verb = *new meaning*
>
> tʃǎn + **dâai** + rúu = *I have discovered*

when **dâai** ได้ is placed before the main verb, it plays the role of a helping verb and its semantic boundaries are also defined by the other verb.

here, **dâai** ได้ goes together with the word **rúu** รู้ *to know*. The meaning **dâai-rúu** ได้ รู้ *get-know* becomes in English *to discover*.

> 2. Subject + **dâai** + a special verb combination = *passive voice in English*
>
> tʃǎn + **dâai** + ráp + tʃɔɔn = *I am invited...* or *I was invited...*

In this sentence, **dâai-ráp** ได้ รับ *to receive* before the verb **tʃɔɔn** เชิญ *to invite* is best translated into English as a passive voice, *I was invited.* For Thais, this is a normal active sentence. Thai people think in terms of *"getting"* or *receiving* the action of *inviting*.

D. Conclusion

> Key: **dâai** ได้ can be placed before verbs in Thai as we already have learned in the previous Secret 5.
>
> With some special verbs when **dâai** ได้ is placed before the main verb, it changes the meaning of the main verb. These are special cases that are born of the usage of language for hundreds of years. They need to be learned by heart.

1. Often **dâai-ráp** ได้ รับ *to receive* before the action verb is translated into English as a passive voice which is much more common in English than in Thai.

2. On the other hand, when **dâai** ได้ is placed before some ordinary action verbs, the translation into English refers to meanings like *"getting" to* or *getting a chance* or *an opportunity to* perform the action in question.

E. Language hints

Here, we would like to give some more examples of **dâai** ได้ being used in compound constructions. We also would like to compare the English passive voice with the Thai style passive voice.

A) First, a few more of sentences with **dâai** ได้ in the compound construction.

> yàak-dâai-ráp อยาก ได้ รับ to want to receive
>
> I *want to receive* a bachelor's degree
>
> อยาก ได้ รับ ปริญญาตรี
> *yàak-dâai-ráp* pàrinyaa-trii
> *want-get-receive* degree-three

yàak-dâai-ráp อยาก ได้ รับ *to want to receive* is a more formal way to express receiving. It is commonly used for things like academic degrees etc.

Secret 6

2 yàak-dâai อยาก ได้ to want

I *want* ice cream

อยาก ได้ ไอติม
yàak *dâai* aitim
want *get* ice cream

If you want to get ice cream, you would not normally use **yàak-dâai** อยาก ได้ *to want, to want to get* instead of **yàak-dâai-ráp** อยาก ได้ รับ *to want to receive*. That would be too formal and sounds odd. Compare this sentence with the sentence 1.

3 To realise, to understand – dâai-khít ได้ คิด

I *have realised* that good-looking men are always flirty/flirtatious.

ฉัน ได้ คิด ว่า ผู้ชาย หล่อ เจ้าชู้ เสมอ
tʃán *dâai-khít* wâa phûu-tʃaai lɔ̀ɔ tsâu-tʃúu sàmɤ̌ɤ
I *get-think* that person-man handsome person-flirt very always

3.1 Alternative way to express the same

I *have realised* that good-looking men are always flirty/flirtatious.

ฉัน เข้า ใจ แล้ว ว่า ผู้ชาย หล่อ เจ้าชู้ เสมอ
tʃán *khâu-tsai* lɛ́ɛu wâa phûu-tʃaai lɔ̀ɔ tsâu-tʃúu sàmɤ̌ɤ
I *enter-heart* already that person-man handsome person-flirt very always

khâu-tsai เข้า ใจ *to understand, to realise* is more common and can be used instead of **dâai-khít** ได้ คิด *to realise, to understand*.

B) English style passive voice

It is often said that Thai people use a passive voice mainly for negative statements only. However, when **dâai-ráp** ได้ รับ is placed before the action verb, the sentence is often best translated into English as the passive voice. Thai people may not think that it is a passive voice. The sentence is just often more conveniently translated into English as a passive voice.

Consider the following:

dâai-ráp ได้ รับ before a noun *to get, to receive*

---

1 Wanting to get – yàak-dâai ráp อยาก ได้ รับ

1.1 I *want to get* a tablet.

ฉัน อยาก ได้ รับ แท็บเล็ต
tʃǎn *yàak-dâai-ráp* théplèt
I *want-get-receive* tablet

Here, **dâai-ráp** ได้ รับ is placed before a concrete noun and the sentence is best translated into English as an active voice.

English active voice: *I want to get a tablet.*

Thai style active voice: *I want to get a tablet.*

The structure is the same in both languages.

1.2 I *want to be* loved.

ฉัน อยาก ได้ รับ ความ รัก
tʃǎn *yàak-dâai-ráp* khwaam-rák
I *want-get-receive* matter-love

We have placed **dâai-ráp** ได้ รับ before an abstract noun **khwaam-rák** ความ รัก *love*.

English passive voice: *I want to be loved.*

This sentence is best expressed in English as a passive voice.

The literal translation into English would be *I want to get love.* It sounds a bit odd in English. However, this is more of a Thai way to think about this action.

> **2**   **dâai-ráp** ได้ รับ before a verb

> **2.1**   I *was invited* to go to study in Singapore
> ผม ได้ รับ เชิญ ให้ ไป เรียน ที่ สิงคโปร์
> phŏm *dâai-ráp ʧɔɔn* hâi pai riian thîi sĭngkhápoo
> I *get-receive invite* for go study at Singapore

Here, **dâai-ráp** ได้ รับ is placed before a verb **ʧɔɔn** เชิญ *to invite*.

English passive voice: *I was invited to go to study.*

This sentence is best translated into English as a passive voice.

The literal translation into English would be *I received an invitation to go to study* which is active voice in Thai. This is more of a Thai way to think about this action.

> **2.2**   I *invited* him to go to study in Singapore.
> ผม ได้ เชิญ เขา ไป เรียน ที่ สิงคโปร์
> phŏm *dâai-ʧɔɔn* kháu pai riian thîi sĭngkhápoo
> I *get-invite* he go study at Singapore

Here, we have placed **dâai** ได้ before a verb **tʃɔɔn** เชิญ *to invite* and dropped the verb **ráp** รับ *to receive*. The grammatical meaning changes.

English active voice: *I invited him to go to study in Singapore.*

This is an active sentence and cannot really be translated into English as a passive voice. It sounds a bit odd to say *he was invited by me to go to study in Singapore*.

The literal translation into English would be *I "got" inviting him to go to study in Singapore*. This is more like a Thai way to think about this action.

> **3** Our proposal *was approved.*
> ข้อ เสนอ ของ เรา ได้ รับ การ อนุมัติ
> khɔ̂ɔ-sànəə khɔ̌ɔng rau *dâai-ráp gaan-ànúmát*
> proposal of we *get-receive approval*

Here, **dâai-ráp** ได้ รับ is placed before an abstract noun **gaan-ànúmát** การ อนุมัติ *approval*.

English passive voice: *Our proposal was approved.*

This sentence is best translated into English as a passive voice.

The literal translation into English would be *our proposal received an approval*.

This is more like a Thai way to think about this action.

Secret 6

Our proposal *was approved* by him.

เขา อนุมัติ ข้อ เสนอ ของ เรา
kháu *ànúmát* khôɔ-sànɤ̌ɤ khɔ̌ɔng rau
he *approve* proposal of we

English passive voice: *Our proposal was approved by him.*

English active voice: *He approved our proposal.*

Here, English could easily use either an active or a passive voice.

The Thai way to think about this is as an active voice, *he approved our proposal.*

Your telephone *will be returned* tomorrow.

พรุ่งนี้ คุณ จะ ได้ โทรศัพท์ คืน
phrûng-níi khun *tsà-dâai thoorásàp khɯɯn*
tomorrow-this you *will-get telephone return*

The above English sentence is usually expressed in Thai as an active voice, *you will get back your telephone tomorrow,* **khun tsà-dâai thoorásàp khɯɯn** คุณ จะ ได้ โทรศัพท์ คืน.

Here, English could easily use either the Active or the passive voice.

English passive voice: *Your telephone will be returned tomorrow.*

English active voice: *You will get back your telephone tomorrow.*

 The Thai style passive voice
doon โดน and **thùuk** ถูก

> The Thai style passive voice is usually expressed by **thùuk** ถูก or **doon** โดน verbs. They are usually interchangeable. The passive voice is mainly used for negative action in Thai.

It is gramatically correct to make Thai style passive sentences into active sentences. However, Thais often prefer to express types of negative activity such as *being robbed, arrested, raped, injured* etc. with the passive voice. In these situations, the subject usually does not have any control of the situation.

Word order in Thai:

> Subject + **doon** or **thùuk** + agent + verb
> = *passive voice*
>
> tʃán + **doon** or **thùuk** + tamrùuat + tsàp
> = *I was arrested by the police.*

In English, we place the word *by* before the agent who carried out the action. In Thai, we may use either **doon** โดน or **thùuk** ถูก.

Note that in other contexts, **doon** โดน also means *to touch* or *to hit* and **thùuk** ถูก means *to touch, to be correct, right, cheap* or *inexpensive*.

Consider the following:

> He *was caught*.
> เขา โดน จับ
> kháu *doon tsàp*
> he *doon catch*

This is the passive voice without an agent carrying out the action.

The helping verb **doon** โดน is placed before the main verb **tsàp** จับ *to catch*.

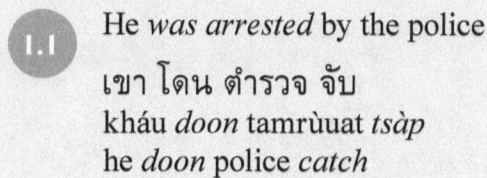

> **1.1** He *was arrested* by the police.
> เขา โดน ตำรวจ จับ
> kháu *doon* tamrùuat *tsàp*
> he *doon* police *catch*

This is a passive voice sentence with an agent.

The agent, **tamrùuat** ตำรวจ *police,* carried out the action. The helping verb **doon** โดน is placed before the agent, and the main verb **tsàp** จับ *to catch* is placed at the end of the sentence.

> **1.2** The police *arrested* him.
> ตำรวจ จับ เขา
> tamrùuat *tsàp* kháu
> police *catch* he

This is an active voice sentence.

However, Thais would prefer to use a passive voice for sentences like this. Compare this sentence with the sentence 1.1 above.

> **2** Yesterday, I *was robbed*.
> เมื่อวาน ฉัน ถูก ขโมย
> mûua-waan tʃán *thùuk khàmooi*
> yesterday, I *thùuk steal*

This a passive voice without an agent.

The helping verb **thùuk** ถูก is placed before the main verb **khàmooi** ขโมย *to steal*.

> **2.1** Yesterday, I *was robbed* by a thief.
> เมื่อวาน ฉัน ถูก โจร ปล้น
> mûɨa-waan tʃán *thùuk tsoon plôn*
> Yesterday, I *thùuk thief rob*

This is a passive voice with the agent **tsoon** โจร *thief* who carried out the action.

The helping verb **thùuk** ถูก is placed before the agent, and the main verb **plôn** ปล้น *to rob* is placed at the end of the sentence.

> **2.2** Yesterday, a thief *robbed* me.
> เมื่อวาน โจร ปล้น ฉัน
> mûɨa-waan tsoon *plôn* tʃán
> Yesterday, thief *rob* I

This sentence is an active voice.

This sentence is grammatically correct but not likely to be used by Thais. In cases like this, Thais would prefer a passive voice as in the sentence 2.1.

F. Simple advice

> We have previously learned that **dâai** ได้ can be placed in different places in the sentence.

In order to get the correct meaning, the following summary may be helpful.

1. When **dâai** ได้ is placed before a concrete noun, the meaning is simply *to get, to receive, to obtain* something. See more about this in Secret 1.

2. When **dâai** ได้ is placed before an abstract noun, it can *change a noun into a verb* as far as the English translation is concerned. The Thai expression **dâai-lâap** ได้ ลาภ *to get luck* becomes *to be lucky*. See more about this in Secret 2.

3. When **dâai** ได้ is placed after the main verb, it is used as a helping verb and can be translated into English as *can, being able to, being allowed to* or *permitted to* do something. See more about this in Secret 3.

4. When **dâai** ได้ is placed before an adjective, it turns an adjective into an *adverb* as far as the English translation is concerned, **dii** ดี *good* becomes *well* etc. See more about this in Secret 4.

5. When **dâai** ได้ is put before the main verb, it is used as a helping verb and can be translated into English as *"getting" to, getting an opportunity to* or *a chance to* do something. See more about this in Secret 5.

6. **dâai** ได้ can also be placed before some special verbs to form a new meaning as demonstrated in this Secret.

☙

3. dâai ได้ and idiomatic expressions

dâai ได้ can be used in many different ways in other idiomatic expressions and therefore the word order can be different.

Secret 7	dâai ได้ and idiomatic expressions I (dâai lé sămnuuan ได้ และ สำนวน I)
Secret 8	dâai ได้ and idiomatic expressions II (dâai lé sămnuuan ได้ และ สำนวน II)

Secret 7

dâai has a way to protect herself. **dâai** says: "Don't take anything personally."

ได้ มี วิธี ปกป้อง ตัว เอง – ได้ บอก ว่า – อย่า ได้ รับ เอา คำ พูด ของ ผู้ อื่น มา เป็น เรื่อง ของ ตัว เอง

dâai mii wíthii pòk-pôŋg tuua-eeng – **dâai** bɔ̀ɔk wâa – yàa-dâai ráp au kham-phûut khɔ̌ɔng phûu-ùɯn maa pen rɯ̂ɯang khɔ̌ɔng tuua-eeng

dâai have way protect-cover body-self – **dâai** say that – no get-receive word-speak of person-other come be story of body-self

dâai ได้ and idiomatic expressions I
(dâai lɛ́ sămnuuan ได้ และ สำนวน I)

dâai ได้ plays a significant role in many different kinds of everyday expressions. It is often used together with other words in an idiomatic way to convey different meanings.

A. Sentences with dâai ได้ and idiomatic expressions I

1 Possible, can be done – pen-pai-dâai เป็น ไป ได้

I think it *is possible*.

ฉัน คิด ว่า เป็น ไป ได้
tʃán khít wâa *pen-pai-dâai*
I think that *be-go-can*

2 Acceptable, moderate, OK, not bad
– phɔɔ-pai-dâai พอ ไป ได้

His work *is acceptable, not too bad*.

งาน เขา พอ ไป ได้
ngaan kháu *phɔɔ-pai-dâai*
Work he *enough-go-can*

3 OK, so so, not bad! – phɔɔ-tʃái-dâai พอ ใช้ ได้

This computer *is OK, not bad!*

คอมพิวเตอร์ เครื่องนี้ พอ ใช้ ได้
khɔɔmphíutə̂ə khrʉ̂ɯang níi *phɔɔ-tʃái-dâai*
Computer-machine this *enough-use-can*

4 To trust someone – wái-tsai dâai ไว้ ใจ ได้

I *can trust* him.

ฉัน ไว้ ใจ เขา ได้
tʃán *wái-tsai* kháu *dâai*
I *keep-heart* he *can*

5 To be trusted – wái-tsai-dâai ไว้ ใจ ได้

He *can be* trusted.

เขา ไว้ ใจ ได้
kháu *wái-tsai-dâai*
He *keep-heart-can*

6 Can't be used, useless – tʃái-mâi-dâai ใช้ ไม่ ได้

This work is *useless*.

งาน นี้ ใช้ ไม่ ได้
ngaan níi *tʃái-mâi-dâai*
Work this *use-no-can*

7 Not getting along – pai-kan-mâi-dâai ไป กัน ไม่ ได้

They *don't get along*.

พวก เขา ไป กัน ไม่ ได้
phûuak-kháu *pai-kan-mâi-dâai*
Group-he *go-together-no-can*

B. Highlights

In the above idiomatic phrases **dâai** ได้ is placed as a last word in the compound phrase. The meaning indicates that the action *is possible, OK, fairly good, not bad, it can be done* etc. **dâai** ได้ can also be placed at the beginning or in the middle of a compound phrase and the meaning is usually different. See more about this in the Language hints section E.

Here is the summary of the above sentences:

pen-pai-dâai	เป็น ไป ได้	to be possible, can be done
phɔɔ-pai-dâai	พอ ไป ได้	fairly good, not bad, acceptable
phɔɔ-tʃái-dâai	พอ ใช้ ได้	OK, not bad, so so
wái-tsai-dâai	ไว้ ใจ ได้	to trust, can be trusted, trustworthy
tʃái-mâi-dâai	ใช้ ไม่ ได้	can't be used, useless
pai-kan-dâai	ไป กัน ได้	to get along well
pai-kan-mâi-dâai	ไป กัน ไม่ ได้	not to get along well

C. Understanding dâai ได้

Generally, **dâai** ได้ can be understood as expressing a positive state of affairs, something that is possible.

Word order:

idiomatic phrase + **dâai** = *special meaning*

pen + pai + **dâai** = *It can be done.*

These idiomatic expressions do not necessarily follow any firm grammatical rules.

In this Secret, we have used the pattern where **dâai** ได้ is placed as the last word in the idiomatic phrase. The meaning is *to be possible*.

These types of positive expressions are usually negated by placing the word **mâi** ไม่ before the verb **dâai** ได้ as follows:

pen-pai mâi-dâai	เป็น ไป ไม่ ได้	it is not possible
wái-tsai mâi-dâai	ไว้ ใจ ไม่ ได้	can't be trusted
tʃái mâi-dâai	ใช้ ไม่ ได้	can't be used

dâai ได้ can be used in many different ways in other idiomatic expressions and therefore the word order can be different. See more about this in the Language hints section E.

D. Conclusion

> Key: Place **dâai** ได้ as the last word in an idiomatic phrase as shown to form idiomatic expressions that usually refer to the *possibility of action*.

1. All idiomatic expressions are special and unique. These expressions should be learned by heart since they don't necessary follow normal grammar rules.

2. When **dâai** ได้ is used in an idiomatic way together with other words, its semantic boundaries are defined by other words and the context. The meaning is born by the usage of the language for many hundreds of years. Each group of words has a specific, unique meaning.

3. When **dâai** ได้ is used in idiomatic expressions, the sentence tends to reflect the present tense.

Example:

> It can be done.
> เป็น ไป ได้
> pen-pai-dâai
> be-go-can

4. We shall give you more of taste of **dâai** ได้ when it is used in idiomatic expressions in the following Language hints section and in the next Secret 8.

E. Language hints

> We give here a few more expressions where **dâai** ได้ is used with different words in an idiomatic way to express several special meanings.
>
> These expressions are used differently compared to the sentences above where **dâai** ได้ is exclusively placed at the end of the expression.

Examples:

> dâai-nâa ได้ หน้า
> His *ego is boosted.*
> เขา ได้ หน้า
> kháu *dâai-nâa*
> he *get-face*

This is an idiomatic expression used in situations when someone is praised for his doings. He feels good, and his *ego is boosted.*

Thai people say *he gets face*. This expression can be used with both positive and negative meanings. However, it is usually used as a negative expression meaning his *ego is boosted*. The positive meaning would be his *prestige is boosted*.

> **1.1** sĭia-nâa เสีย หน้า
>
> He *lost face*.
>
> เขา เสีย หน้า
> kháu *sĭia-nâa*
> he *lose-face*

The opposite for **dâai-nâa** ได้ หน้า is **sĭia-nâa** เสีย หน้า *to lose face*.

> **2** yàa dâai-nâa อย่า ได้ หน้า
>
> *Don't be overconfident.*
>
> อย่า ได้ หน้า ไป เลย
> *yàa dâai-nâa pai-ləəi*
> *do not get-face go-sure*

This expression has a similar meaning as **yàa dâai-tsai** อย่า ได้ ใจ *don't be overconfident*. These expressions are negative but can be used in a playful way with friends.

> **2.1** yàa wôə อย่า เว่อร์
>
> *Don't overdo it!*
>
> อย่า เว่อร์
> *yàa wôə*
> *don't over*

This is a similar expression compared to the previous sentence 2.

> **3** dâai-nâa dâai-taa ได้ หน้า ได้ ตา
> *To gain popularity.*
>
> ได้ หน้า ได้ ตา
> dâai-nâa dâai-taa
> get-face get-eye

This can also be understood as *getting favour*.

> **4** dâai-nâa luum-lăng ได้ หน้า ลืม หลัง
> He *forgets everything.*
>
> เขา ได้ หน้า ลืม หลัง
> kháu *dâai-nâa luum-lăng*
> He *get-next forget-later*

This expression is usually used in a negative way.

Here, **dâai-nâa** ได้ หน้า is used in the sense of "future time", *next moment*. This kind of person forgets everything the next moment.

nâa หน้า has several meanings such as *face, front, next*.

Another expression that Thai people may use in a similar situation is **khîi-luum** ขี้ ลืม *to be forgetful*.

> **5** tsà-dâai mái จะ ได้ ไหม
> *Is it possible?*
>
> จะ ได้ ไหม
> tsà-dâai mái
> will-can question

This type of idiomatic expression is used when asking questions. This is similar to **pen-pai-dâi-mái** เป็น ไป ได้ ไหม *Is it possible? Is it OK?*

> **6** *Whatever comes easy, goes easy!*
> ได้ มา ง่าย ก็ เสีย ไป ง่าย
> *dâai-maa ngâai kɔ̂ɔ sĭia pai ngâai*
> get-come easy also lose go easy

dâai-maa ได้ มา means *to get, to acquire.*

> **7** To get it – dâai-kaan ได้ การ
> *I got it!*
> ได้ การ แล้ว
> *dâai-kaan-lɛ́ɛu*
> get-task already

dâai-kaan lɛ́ɛu ได้ การ แล้ว means *to get the meaning, to resolve the problem, to understand* or *to find the way!*

The literal translation into English would be *I got the task already.*

kaan การ *task, work, job* is used in many different ways in the Thai language.

> **8** Another way to say "not bad"
> *It is not bad!*
> ไม่ เลว
> *mâi leeu*
> not bad

Another way to say *not bad, fairly good* is to use the word **leeu** เลว *bad* and negate it, **mâi leeu** ไม่ เลว *not bad*.

However, the colour of the statement is different compared to **phɔɔ-pai-dâai** พอ ไป ได้ *fairly good, not bad, acceptable* or **phɔɔ-tʃái-dâai** พอ ใช้ ได้ *OK, not bad, so so*.

F. Simple advice

Many expressions in Thai, as in any other language, have been born by the usage of the language over many hundreds of years. Often there is no grammatical reason why certain words are used together to form new meanings. There is no other way to get these idiomatic expressions right than by learning them by heart.

> Idiomatic expressions with **dâai** ได้ can be very useful when interacting with Thai people. Knowing how to use them well shows that your command of the Thai language is more advanced than just being able to express basic simple meanings. You will be able to express the subtleties and complexity of different meanings.

Learn as many idiomatic expressions with **dâai** ได้ as possible. These expressions are fun, and Thai people use them a lot. If you are able to use at least a few of the most common idiomatic expressions with **dâai** ได้ correctly, it shows that you can speak Thai as Thai people do.

Secret 8

dâai is well educated and she knows a lot about life. **dâai** says: "There is no need to speak about everything you know and see. Sometimes it is better to be quiet and smile. That saves you from many kinds of trouble."

ได้ มี ความ รู้ เยอะ และ เข้า ใจ ชีวิต มาก – ได้ บอก ว่า – ไม่ จำ เป็น ต้อง พูด ถึง ทุก อย่าง ที่ คุณ รู้ และ เห็น – บาง ครั้ง อยู่ เงียบๆ และ ยิ้ม จะ ดี กว่า – วิธี นี้ จะ ป้อง กัน ตัว เอง จาก ปัญหา หลาย เรื่อง

dâai mii khwaam-rúu yɤ́ lέ khâu-tsai tʃii-wít mâak – **dâai** bɔ̀ɔk-wâa – mâi tsam-pen-tông phûut thŭng thúk-yàang thîi khun rúu lέ hĕn – baang-khráng yùu ngîiap-ngîiap lέ yím tsà dii kwàa – wíthii níi tsà pông kan tuua-eeng tsàak lăai panhăa lăai rûɯang

dâai have matter-know much and enter-heart life much – **dâai** say that – no need-be-must speak-reach every-kind that you know and see – some-time stay quiet and smile will good more – method this will protect with body-self from many problem many trouble

dâai ได้ and more idiomatic expressions II
(dâai lɛ́ sămnuuan ได้ และ สำนวน II)

Idiomatic expression with **dâai** ได้ are so important that we have decided to take two separate Secrets just for them. **dâai** ได้ is regularly used with many common expressions such as **arai-kɔ̃ɔ-dâai** อะไร ก็ ได้ *anything, whatever, as you like,* **dâai-weelaa-lɛ́ɛu** ได้ เวลา แล้ว *it is time to... , time is up,* **yùt dâai-lɛ́ɛu** หยุด ได้ แล้ว *stop it, will you!*

A. Sentences with dâai ได้ and idiomatic expressions II

1 Anything is fine – kɔ̂ɔ-dâai ก็ ได้

Whatever you like – arai kɔ̂ɔ-dâai อะไร ก็ ได้

You can eat *whatever you like*.

คุณ กิน อะไร ก็ ได้
khun kin *arai kɔ̂ɔ-dâai*
you eat *what also-can*

1.1 Whenever you like – mûua-rài kɔ̂ɔ-dâai เมื่อ ไหร่ ก็ ได้

We can go *any time you like!*

ไป เมื่อ ไหร่ ก็ ได้
pai *mûua-rài kɔ̂ɔ-dâai*
go *when-anything also-can*

1.2 Any place you like – thîi-nǎi kɔ̂ɔ-dâai ที่ ไหน ก็ ได้

We can meet *any place you like*.

เจอ กัน ที่ ไหน ก็ ได้
tɕəə-kan *thîi-nǎi kɔ̂ɔ-dâai*
meet-together *place-which also-can*

1.3 As you like – yang-ngai kɔ̂ɔ-dâai ยัง ไง ก็ ได้

Do *as you like*.

ทำ ยัง ไง ก็ ได้
tham *yang-ngai kɔ̂ɔ-dâai*
do as *how also-can*

2 Time is up – dâai... léɛu ได้... แล้ว

He said that *it's time to go.*

เขา บอก ว่า ได้ เวลา ไป แล้ว
kháu bɔ̀ɔk wâa – *dâai-weelaa pai léɛu*
he tell that – *get-time go already*

2.1 Let's go! – pai dâai-léɛu ไป ได้ แล้ว

The bus is coming. *Let's go!*

รถ เมล์ กำลัง มา – ไป ได้ แล้ว
rót-mee kamlang maa – *pai dâai-léɛu*
bus "kamlang" come – *go can-already*

3 Commands: Stop it! – yùt dâai-léɛu หยุด ได้ แล้ว

Don't do it like that! *Stop now!*

อย่า ทำ แบบ นี้ – หยุด ได้ แล้ว
yàa tham bɛ̀ɛp-níi – *yùt dâai-léɛu*
don't do way this – *stop can-already*

3.1 Do it! – tham dâai-léɛu ทำ ได้ แล้ว

We do not have much time. *Do it now!*

เรา ไม่ มี เวลา เยอะ นะ – ทำ ได้ แล้ว
rau mâi mii weelaa yá ná – *tham dâai-léɛu*
we no have time much ná – *do can-already*

3.2 Eat now! – kin dâai-léɛu กิน ได้ แล้ว

The food is ready. *Eat now!*

อาหาร พร้อม แล้ว – กิน ได้ แล้ว ค่ะ
aahǎan phrɔ́ɔm léɛu – *kin dâai-léɛu khâ*
food ready already – *eat can-already khâ*

B. Highlights

> These idiomatic expressions are used somewhat differently. They are used everyday by Thai people in many different combinations.

 kɔ̂ɔ-dâai ก็ได้ is usually placed at end of the statement. It is a sign of being *indifferent, anything is possible*.
kɔ̂ɔ-dâai ก็ได้ can be used with many different kinds of action verbs. It is commonly placed after the following question words like:

arai	อะไร	*what*
mûua-rài	เมื่อไหร่	*when*
thîi-nǎi	ที่ไหน	*where*
yang-ngai	ยังไง	*how*

arai kɔ̂ɔ-dâai อะไร ก็ได้ can be translated into English as *do as you like, I don't really care, whatever is fine*. It is also often used in a situation where one doesn't know what to do or doesn't want to take responsibility for an action. One lets the other person take the responsibility.

mûua-rài kɔ̂ɔ-dâai เมื่อ ไหร่ ก็ ได้ *any time is fine!* can be used to show that one is flexible, and lets the other person choose the *time*.

thîi-nǎi kɔ̂ɔ-dâai ที่ ไหน ก็ ได้ *any place is fine!* can be used with the *location* to show that one is flexible, and lets the other person choose the *place*.

yang-ngai kɔ̂ɔ-dâai ยังไง ก็ ได้ *whatever way you like* can be used to show that one is flexible, and lets the other person decide *how*.

dâai-weelaa-lέεu ได้ เวลา แล้ว *it is time to...*

dâai-weelaa-lέεu ได้ เวลา แล้ว is used in situations *when time is up* or *when it is time to* do something.

dâai-lέεu ได้ แล้ว is a slightly more sophisticated expression. It is placed after the action verb *to give commands* and add some *extra weight* to the action. **dâai-lέεu** ได้ แล้ว can be used with almost any action verb. Depending on the situation, it can be translated somewhat differently.

yùt dâai-lέεu หยุด ได้ แล้ว is a command and means simply *stop it!*

pai dâai-lέεu ไป ได้ แล้ว is translated into English as suggestions *let's go, he may go* or as commands like *go now* or *go away!*

tham dâai-lέεu ทำ ได้ แล้ว as a command means *do it!* In another context, **tham dâai-lέεu** ทำ ได้ แล้ว could also be translated into English as *I did it already* or *let's do it.*

kin dâai-lέεu กิน ได้ แล้ว is a command meaning *eat now!* In another context, it could mean *I have already eaten* or *let's eat!*

C. Understanding dâai ได้

Generally, **dâai** ได้ can be understood as expressing a positive state of affairs, something that is possible.

As we have already learned in the previous Secret 7, **dâai** ได้ can be used together with a number of words in an idiomatic way. There are many examples, and it is impossible to cover all of them here. In this book, we try to give you a taste of **dâai** ได้ and introduce the most common ways in which **dâai** ได้ is used everyday by Thai people.

Word order:

We cannot give a complete overview of the word order here since **dâai** ได้ may be placed in different positions in different idiomatic phrases.

However, often **dâai** ได้ is placed at the end of the idiomatic phrase.

Three common idiomatic expressions with **dâai** ได้.

arai kɔ̂ɔ-dâai อะไร ก็ ได้
– *as you like, anything is fine, anything is possible*

If you ask a Thai person "What would you like to do"? They would probably reply to you **arai kɔ̂ɔ-dâai** อะไร ก็ ได้ *anything is possible, whatever, as you like, I don't really care etc.*

But what does it really mean? Depending on the situation, **arai kɔ̂ɔ-dâai** อะไร ก็ ได้ can also mean *let me hear what you have in mind, let us discuss*. It is used as a neutral introduction before making a decision. They do not want to unveil their real intentions that quick.

This expression is used in many different situations by Thais. It is often used when one doesn't know or doesn't want to know exactly what to do. Then, Thai people would say **arai-kɔ̂ɔ-dâai** อะไร ก็ ได้ *anything is possible*.

All the doors are left open.

The other expression **lɛ́ɛu-tɛ̀ɛ-khun** แล้ว แต่ คุณ *it is up to you* is used in the similar way.

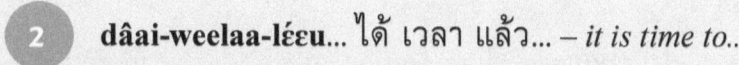

dâai-weelaa-lɛ́ɛu ได้ เวลา แล้ว is used in situations when time is up or when it is time to do something. This could also be translated freely into English as *let's go*.

thǔng-weelaa-lɛ́ɛu ถึง เวลา แล้ว is used in a similar way to **dâai-weelaa-lɛ́ɛu** ได้ เวลา แล้ว. They are often interchangeable.

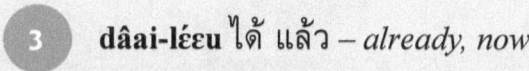

dâai-lɛ́ɛu ได้ แล้ว is used in a number of different situations. It is often used in connection with commands. **dâai-lɛ́ɛu** ได้ แล้ว is placed after the main verb. It makes the meaning of the action verb stronger.

D. Conclusion

> Key: There are a vast number of idiomatic expressions where **dâai** ได้ can be included. It seems that the list is almost endless. It is best to learn them by heart.

1. When **dâai** ได้ is used in an idiomatic way together with other words, its semantic boundaries are defined by other words and the context. The meaning is born by the usage of the language for many hundreds of years. Each group of words has a specific meaning and they do not usually follow normal grammatical rules.

2. **dâai** ได้ is often placed at the end of an idiomatic phrase to express the *possibility of action.* It can, however, be placed before or in the middle of an idiomatic phrase and the meaning can be different.

3. In the next Language hints section, we give you more taste of **dâai** ได้ when it is used in idiomatic expressions.

4. When **dâai** ได้ is used in idiomatic expressions, the sentence tends to reflect the present tense.

> Do as you like!
> อะไร ก็ ได้
> *arai kɔ̂ɔ-dâai*
> *what-also-can*

E. Language hints

Taste of **dâai** ได้ and more idiomatic expressions.

A) Here we introduce a few more idiomatic examples where **dâai** ได้ plays a central role:

> **1** Complaining a lot – phûut-yùu-dâai – bòn-yùu-dâai
> พูด อยู่ ได้ บ่น อยู่ ได้
>
> *You are really complaining!*
>
> พูด อยู่ ได้ – บ่น อยู่ ได้
> *phûut-yùu-dâai – bòn-yùu-dâai*
> *speak-be-can – complain-be-can*

This is one of those few expressions where **dâai** ได้ is included in a negative phrase.

2 Being selfish – au-tὲε-dâai เอา แต่ ได้

He *is being selfish*.

เขา เอา แต่ ได้
kháu *au-tὲε-dâai*
he *take-but-get*

This is another expression where **dâai** ได้ is included in a negative phrase.

3 Whatever happens – hâi-dâai ให้ ได้

I will go *whatever happens*!

ผม จะ ไป ให้ ได้
phŏm tsà pai *hâi-dâai*
I will go *give-can*

hâi-dâai ให้ ได้ is used in the special idiomatic way. See more about how Thai uses the verb **hâi** ให้ in the book *Learning Thai with hâi* ให้ – *22 Secrets of Learning Thai*.

4 Until finished – tson-dâai จน ได้

I will do it *until finished*.

จะ ทำ จน ได้
tsà tham *tson-dâai*
will do *until-get*

tson-dâai จน ได้ can also be translated into English as *until I get it*.

> **5** Having had sex – dâai-sĭia-kan lɛ́ɛu ได้ เสีย กัน แล้ว
>
> They *already had sex*.
>
> พวก เขา ได้ เสีย กัน แล้ว
> phûuak-kháu *dâai-sĭia-kan lɛ́ɛu*
> group-he *get-loose-together already*

dâai-sĭia-kan lɛ́ɛu ได้ เสีย กัน แล้ว is usually used only when referring to the sex act.

> **6** Being successful – dâai-dìp dâai-dii ได้ ดิบ ได้ ดี
>
> He *is successful*.
>
> เขา ได้ ดิบ ได้ ดี
> kháu *dâai-dìp dâai-dii*
> he *get-raw get-good*

dâai-dìp dâai-dii ได้ ดิบ ได้ ดี *being successful* is a special expression which may not be used much in everyday speaking.

Note that in the above six sentences we have given a word for word translation of **dâai** ได้ which sometimes means *can* and sometimes *to get*. The difference is very subtle and goes beyond the explanation here. It has to do with the feeling, and which of the two is considered more natural.

B) Alternative ways to express *let's go*

Earlier, in this Secret, we have pointed out that the English phrase *let's go* can be expressed in Thai with phrases like **pai dâai-lɛ́ɛu** ไป ได้ แล้ว *let's go,* **dâai-weelaa-lɛ́ɛu** ได้ เวลา แล้ว *it is time to, time is up*.

There are some other ways to express a similar meaning in Thai.

Consider the following:

> **1**
> thŭng-weelaa-lɛ́ɛu ถึง เวลา แล้ว
>
> He said that *it is time to go.*
>
> เขา บอก ว่า – ถึง เวลา ไป แล้ว
> kháu bɔ̀ɔk wâa – *thŭng-weelaa pai-lɛ́ɛu*
> he tell that – *arrive-time go-already*

thŭng-weelaa-lɛ́ɛu... ถึง เวลา แล้ว *it is time to, the time is up*

Here, **dâai** ได้ is replaced by **thŭng** ถึง. **thŭng-weelaa-lɛ́ɛu** ถึง เวลา แล้ว is used in a similar way.

> **2**
> pai-kan-thɔ̀ ไป กัน เถอะ
>
> *Let's go!*
>
> ไป กัน เถอะ
> *pai-kan-thɔ̀*
> *go-together-thɔ̀*

pai-kan-thɔ̀ ไป กัน เถอะ *let's go!*

This expression is more direct than the previous one.

pai-kan-thɔ̀ ไป กัน เถอะ *let's go!* **thɔ̀** เถอะ is an intensifier that expresses some urge to do an action. It has no direct translation into English. The closest we can come to is *let's*.

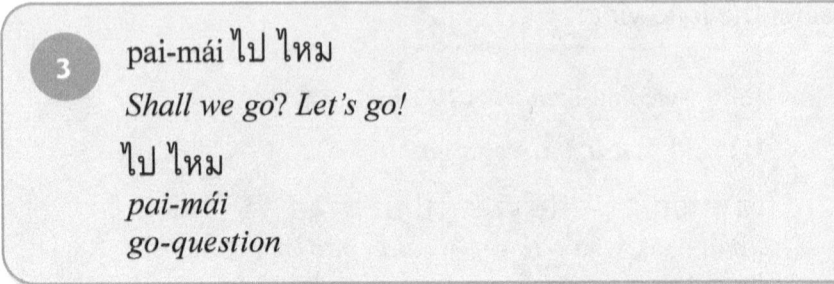

pai-mái ไป ไหม *shall we go?*

Thai people often use the question word **pai-mái** ไป ไหม *Shall we go? Are you ready?* The meaning is very similar to the English phrase *let's go!*

This is very polite since it allows space for the other person to decide.

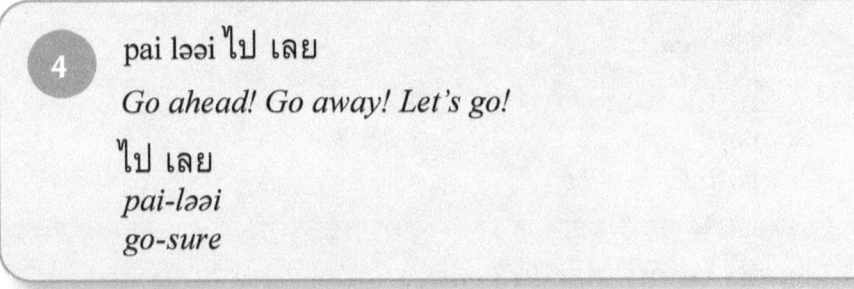

pai-ləəi ไป เลย *Let's go! Go away!*

One should be a little careful when using this expression since it can very rude if used in the wrong way or in the wrong situation. It can also be offensive when used with somebody you don't know. This expression is best used only in a playful way with friends.

ləəi เลย is an intensifier that has several meanings depending on the situation and context. It can be translated into English as *very, sure, excess, beyond, pass* etc.

F. Simple advice

Idiomatic expressions with **dâai** ได้ can be very useful when interacting with Thai people. Knowing how to use them well, you will be able to use language which is more expressive and better conveys your feelings. Your language will become richer.

Using idiomatic expressions is a fun way to enrich your language skills. If you learn to use these expressions well, your daily life in Thailand will become more fun for sure.

> When using idiomatic expressions with **dâai** ได้, it is good to be aware of the context and to whom you are speaking. Some phrases are more suitable for using with friends. Some expressions can be fine in one situation and offensive in another situation. This requires some sensitivity on your part.

4. dâai ได้ and asking permission and giving permission

dâai ได้ may be used to transform direct questions into a softer form of request, which is an easy way to express politeness and gratitude in Thai.

dâai ได้ is also commonly used as a part of a reply when giving permission.

> **Secret 9**   dâai ได้ and asking permission
> (dâai lé kaan khɔ̌ɔ anúyâat
> ได้ และ การ ขอ อนุญาต)
>
> **Secret 10**   dâai ได้ and giving permission
> (dâai lé kaan anúyâat hâi
> ได้ และ การ อนุญาต ให้)

Secret 9

dâai is a very curious person. She wants to know many different kinds of things. **dâai** says: "We must be brave enough to ask. If we do not ask, we do not know."

ได้ เป็น คน ที่ อยาก รู้ อยาก เห็น – เธอ อยาก รู้ หลาย สิ่ง หลาย อย่าง – ได้ บอก ว่า – เรา ต้อง กล้า พอ ที่ จะ ถาม – ถ้า ไม่ ถาม เรา ก็ จะ ไม่ รู้

dâai pen khon thîi yàak rúu yàak hĕn – thəə yàak rúu lăai sìng lăai yàang – dâai bɔ̀ɔk wâa – rau tɔ̂ng klâa phɔɔ thîi tsà thăam – thâa mâi thăam rau kɔ̂ɔ tsà mâi rúu

dâai is person that want-know want-see – she want know many thing many kind – **dâai** say that – we must brave enough that will ask – if not ask we also no know

dâai ได้ and asking for permission

dâai ได้ plays an important role when asking questions or when making a request. **dâai-mái** ได้ ไหม at the end of the sentence is also a very good phrase which makes a demand sound like a polite question.

A. Sentences with dâai ได้ asking for permission and questions

I May I, can I, could I questions?
– dâai-mái
ได้ ไหม

1.1 *May I* do it like this?

ทำ แบบ นี้ ได้ ไหม คะ
tham bὲɛp-níi *dâai-mái* khá
Do kind-this *can-question* khá

1.2 *Can we* be friends?

เรา เป็น เพื่อน กัน ได้ ไหม
rau pen phʉ̂ʉan-kan *dâai-mái*
we be friend *can-question*

1.3 *Could you* help me a little?

ช่วย ฉัน หน่อย ได้ ไหม คะ
tʃûuai tʃán nɔ̀i *dâai-mái* khá
help I little *can-question* khá

1.4 *Please*, don't do it like this!

อย่า ทำ แบบ นี้ ได้ ไหม คะ
yàa tham bὲɛp-níi *dâai-mái* khá
no do kind-this *can-question* khá

2 Can or not questions? – dâai-rŭ-plàu ได้ รึ เปล่า

2.1 *Can* I do it like this *or not*?

ทำ แบบ นี้ ได้ รึ เปล่า
tham bɛ̀ɛp-níi *dâai-rŭ-plàu*
do kind-this *can-or-not*

2.2 *Can* he go *or not*?

เขา ไป ได้ รึ เปล่า
kău pai *dâai-rŭ-plàu*
he go *can-or-not*

2.3 *Can* you hurry up a little *or not*!

คุณ รีบ หน่อย ได้ รึ เปล่า
khun rîip nɔ̀i *dâai-rŭ-plàu*
you fast-little *can-or-not*

3 Where questions? – dâai-thîi-năi ได้ ที่ ไหน

Where can we go?

จะ ไป ได้ ที่ ไหน คะ
tsà pai *dâai-thîi-năi* khá
will go *can-place-which* khá

4 When questions? dâai-mûua-rài ได้ เมื่อ ไหร่

When can I buy it?

จะ ซื้อ ได้ เมื่อ ไหร่ คะ
tsà súu *dâai-mûua-rài* khá
will buy *can-when* khá

5 How questions? dâai-yang-ngai ได้ ยังไง

How can I do it?

จะ ทำ ได้ ยังไง
tsà tham *dâai-yang-ngai*
will do *can-how*

6 Who questions? – khrai... dâai ใคร... ได้

Who will *be able to* come?

ใคร จะ มา ได้
khrai tsà maa *dâai*
who will come *can*

7 Why questions? – thammai... dâai ทำไม... ได้

Why can you go, but I *can't*?

ทำไม คุณ ไป ได้ แต่ ฉัน ไป ไม่ ได้
thammai khun pai *dâai* tɛ̀ɛ tʃán pai *mâi-dâai*
why you go *can* but I go *no-can*

B. Highlights

dâai ได้ plays an important part when asking simple basic questions.

Secret 9

 A) **dâai** ได้ can be placed before a question word in order to form a polite question, a request or even a command. Two common question words in Thai are **mái** ไหม and **rŭ-plàu** รึ เปล่า *or not* questions that are placed at the end of the sentence.

 dâai-mái ได้ ไหม *may I, can we, could you? Please!*

dâai-mái ได้ ไหม at the end of the statement is a polite way to make a request, ask for help, make a suggestion or even to give a soft command.

Polite request particles **khá** คะ or **kráp** ครับ at the end of a statement are usually used to soften a request or a command.

nɔ̀i หน่อย *a little* is also commonly employed in Thai to make a request sound like it is not a big deal.

See the above sentences 1.1–1.4, page 152.

 dâai-rŭ-plàu ได้ รึ เปล่า *can or not*

dâai-rŭ-plàu ได้ รึ เปล่า usually suggests that one should give a definite reply, *yes* or *no*. It is, therefore, not considered to be as polite as **dâai-mái** ได้ ไหม question.

Often **dâai-rŭ-plàu** ได้ รึ เปล่า statements can be translated into English in more or less the same way as **dâai-mái** ได้ ไหม questions. There is, however, a difference. **dâai-mái** ได้ ไหม questions show more respect while **dâai-rŭ-plàu** ได้ รึ เปล่า is more demanding.

If the statement implies a request, it can be made *softer* by placing **nɔ̀i** หน่อย after the main verb.

See the above sentences 2.1–2.3, page 153.

B) In addition, **dâai** ได้ can be used with several question words to form polite questions as follows:

> **3** Several question words and dâai ได้ before the question word.
>
> | | | |
> |---|---|---|
> | **thîi-năi** | ที่ไหน | *where?* |
> | **dâai-thîi-năi** | ได้ที่ไหน | *where it is possible?* |
> | **mûua-rài** | เมื่อไหร่ | *when?* |
> | **dâai-mûua-rài** | ได้เมื่อไร | *when it is possible?* |
> | **yang-ngai** | ยังไง | *how?* |
> | **dâai-yang-ngai** | ได้ยังไง | *how it is possible?* |

When the question word is at the end of the sentence, **dâai** ได้ is placed directly before the question word.

See the above sentences 3–5, page 153.

C) **dâai** ได้ after the question word

When the question word is at the beginning of the sentence, **dâai** ได้ is placed after the question word and usually at the end of the sentence.

> **4** A few question words and **dâai** ได้ after the question word.
>
> Examples:
>
> | | | |
> |---|---|---|
> | **khrai** | ใคร | *who?* |
> | **khrai... dâai** | ใคร... ได้ | *who is able to?* |
> | **thammai** | ทำไม | *why?* |
> | **thammai... dâai** | ทำไม... ได้ | *why is... able to?* |

See the above sentences 6–7, page 154.

C. Understanding dâai ได้ and asking for permission

Generally, **dâai** ได้ can be understood as expressing a positive state of affairs, something that is possible.

> In this Secret, we have extended the semantic boundaries of **dâai** ได้ to be used as a part of the question in order being able to express politeness and gratitude.
>
> **dâai** ได้ plays an important role when asking questions or when making a request. **dâai-mái** ได้ ไหม at the end of the sentence is also a very good phrase to make a demand sound like a polite question.

In Thai, polite asking and requesting is usually expressed by a question word **dâai-mái** ได้ ไหม *may I, could I, can I*. It is generally softer and more polite than **dâai-rú-plàu** ได้ รึ เปล่า *can or not* question since it does not require a definite answer. **dâai-rú-plàu** ได้ รึ เปล่า questions call for a reply which should be either *yes* or *no*.

Word order:

> 1. subject + verb + **dâai-mái** = *polite question or request*
>
> tʃán + pai + **dâai-mái** = *Can I go?*

> 2. subject + verb + **dâai-rú-plàu** *can or not*
>
> khun + pai + **dâai-rú-plàu** = Can you go or not?

If you want to learn more about question words in Thai see also the pages 233–238 in the book *Learning Thai with hâi* ให้ *– 22 Secrets of Learning Thai.*

1. Some common question words are:

mái	ไหม	*question?*
rú-plàu	รึ เปล่า	*or not?*
thîi-năi	ที่ ไหน	*where?*
yang-ngai	ยังไง	*how?*
mûua-rài	เมื่อ ไหร่	*when?*
khrai	ใคร	*who?*
thammai	ทำไม	*why?*

2. The meaning with **dâai** ได้ becomes as follows:

dâai-mái	ได้ ไหม	*may I, can I, could I?*
dâai-rú-plàu	ได้ รึ เปล่า	*is it possible or not?*
dâai-thîi-năi	ได้ ที่ ไหน	*where it is possible?*
dâai-yang-ngai	ได้ ยังไง	*how it is possible?*
dâai-mûua-rài	ได้ เมื่อ ไหร่	*when it is possible?*

3. With some question words **dâai** ได้ is placed after the question word.

khrai... dâai	ใคร... ได้	*who is able to?*
thammai... dâai	ทำไม... ได้	*why is... able to?*
thammai	ทำไม	*why?*

D. Conclusion

> Key: Place **dâai** ได้ before the question word **mái** ไหม to transform a direct question into a softer form of request as shown above. That is an easy way to express politeness and gratitude.

1. Polite request particles **khá** คะ or **kráp** ครับ at the end of a statement are also frequently used by Thais to soften a request or a command.

2. **nɔ̀i** หน่อย *a little* is also commonly employed in Thai to make a request sound like it is not a big deal.

3. Some question words in Thai can be placed either at the beginning or the end of a sentence.

   When the question word is placed at the beginning of the sentence, then **dâai** ได้ is separated from the question word and placed at the end of the sentence.

Example:

> **1**
>
> mûua-rài เมื่อ ไหร่
> *when* at the beginning of the sentence
>
> *When* are you *able to* go to Phuket?
>
> เมื่อ ไหร่ คุณ จะ ไป ภูเก็ต ได้
> *mûua-rài* khun tsà pai phuukèt *dâai*
> when you will go Phuket can

Here, the question **mûua-rài** เมื่อ ไหร่ is emphasized and is therefore placed at the beginning of the sentence.

> **2**
>
> mûua-rài เมื่อ ไหร่ *when* at the end of the sentence
>
> *When* are you *able to* go to Phuket?
>
> คุณ จะ ไป ภูเก็ต ได้ เมื่อ ไหร่
> khun tsà pai phuukèt *dâai-mûua-rài*
> you will go Phuket can-when

Here, the question **mûua-rài** เมื่อ ไหร่ is placed at the end of the sentence. The emphasis is on *going to Phuket*.

E. Language hints

We have already learned in this section how to make questions when **dâai** ได้ is used as a part of a question.

We shall introduce here a few more ways to ask and reply to questions that are similar to **dâai-mái** ได้ ไหม questions:

> **1** Is it OK – oo-khee-mái โอเค ไหม
>
> *Is it OK* to sit here?
>
> นั่ง ที่ นี่ โอเค ไหม คะ/ครับ
> nâng thîi-nîi *oo-khee-mái* khá/khráp
> sit place-this *OK question* khá/khráp

oo-khee-mái โอเค ไหม *is it OK?* This expression is borrowed from English.

oo-khee-mái โอเค ไหม may be used as an informal question word, usually with friends, instead of the **dâai-mái** ได้ ไหม question which can also be used in formal situations.

> **1.1** Simple reply:
>
> *It is OK.*
>
> โอเค ครับ
> *oo-khee* khráp

This is a reply to the **oo-khee-mái** โอเค ไหม question. When replying to an **oo-khee-mái** โอเค ไหม question, the answer usually contains the word **oo-khee** โอเค *OK.*

1.2 Negative reply:

It is not OK.

ไม่ โอเค ครับ
mâi oo-khee khráp
no oo-khee khráp

This is a negative reply to the **oo-khee-mái** โอเค ไหม question.

2 Is it fine? – dii-mái ดี ไหม

Is it fine to go by bus?

ไป รถ เมล์ ดี ไหม
pai rót-mee *dii-mái*
go car-mail *good-question*

dii-mái ดี ไหม *question word, is it good, is it fine* is usually used with friends only.

dii-mái ดี ไหม question word is sometimes used in Thai instead of **dâai-mái** ได้ ไหม. This is a more informal way to express a request compared to the **dâai-mái** ได้ ไหม question word.

2.1 Simple reply:

Yes, it is fine.

ดี ค่ะ
dii khâ
good khâ

Note that this reply is formulated according to the question, here **dii** ดี *good* is included in the reply.

2.2 Negative reply:

It's *not so* good!

ไม่ ค่อย ดี ค่ะ
mâi khɔ̂ɔi dii khâ
no hardly good khâ

This is a negative reply to the **dii-mái** ดี ไหม question.

2.3 Reply expressing certainty:

Yes, *certainly*.

ดี อยู่ แล้ว ค่ะ
dii-yùu-lɛ́ɛu khâ
good-stay-already khâ

yùu-lɛ́ɛu อยู่ แล้ว is a special expression that is translated here as *certainly, for sure*.

2.4 Alternative reply:

This bus is full but the bus over there is not full.

รถ คัน นี้ ไม่ ว่าง – แต่ รถ คัน นั้น ว่าง ค่ะ
rót-khan-níi *mâi wâang* – tɛ̀ɛ rót-khan-nán wâang khâ
car-vehicle-this *no vacant* – but car-vehicle-that *vacant* khâ

The above two statements 2.3 and 2.4 change the emphasis. The later is an indirect way to reply to the question. Therefore a part of the question is not included in the reply.

> **2.5** Alternative reply:
>
> Sorry, but this bus is completely full!
>
> ขอโทษ นะ คะ – รถ คัน นี้ เต็ม หมด เลย
> khɔ̌ɔ-thôot ná khá – rót-khan-níi tem-mòt-ləəi
> ask-blame – car-vehicle-this *full-entire-sure*

> **3** Where questions? – thîi-nǎi-dii ที่ ไหน ดี
>
> *Where can* we go?
>
> ไป ที่ ไหน ดี
> pai *thîi-nǎi-dii*
> go *place-which-good*

thîi-nǎi-dii ที่ ไหน ดี *where is good?*

This question is often used in Thai when asking the question *where can I sit?* It is used in other situations as well. It is often used in Thai instead of **dâai-thîi-nǎi** ได้ ที่ ไหน *where is it possible?*.

> **3.1** Simple reply:
>
> We can go *anywhere you like*.
>
> ไป ไหน ก็ ดี ครับ
> pai nǎi *kɔ̂ɔ-dii* khráp
> place-which *also-good* khráp

The reply is formulated according to the question, here **dii** ดี *good* is included in the reply.

4. Like this OK? – bèɛp-níi oo-khee mái แบบนี้ โอเค ไหม

Is it OK to do it *like this*?

ทำ แบบนี้ โอเค ไหม
tham *bèɛp-níi oo-khee mái*
do *like-this OK question*

4.1 Simple reply:

OK, go ahead!

โอเค ทำ ไป เลย ครับ
oo-khee *tham-pai-ləəi* khráp
OK *do-go-sure* khráp

tham-pai-ləəi ทำ ไป เลย *Do it!*, *Go ahead!* is used in the similar way as **dâai-ləəi** ได้ เลย *for sure* or **dâai-yùu-lɛ́ɛu** ได้ อยู่ แล้ว *certainly* to tell a person that it is possible *for sure*.

5. Question word – mái ไหม

Let's be friends!

เรา เป็น เพื่อน กัน ไหม คะ/ครับ
rau pen phûɯan kan *mái* khá/khráp
we be friend *question* khá/khráp

The **mái** ไหม question word is a simple direct question.

When **dâai** ได้ is dropped, the statement turns into a simple question or suggestion. This sentence could also be translated into English as *can we be friends* or *are we friends*?

F. Simple advice

Everything becomes much easier in Thailand if you are able to express yourself politely. In fact, it is almost impossible to be too polite in Thailand.

> When asking for permission or making a request, **dâai** ได้ plays a significant role in being polite. The request can be made *softer* by putting the question word **dâai-mái** ได้ไหม *may I, could I, can I* at the end of the sentence. **nɔ̀i** หน่อย *little* can also be used to show politeness on your part. In addition, polite request particles such as **ná, khá, khâ, khráp** นะ คะ ค่ะ ครับ are commonly used by all Thai people.

Thai people usually judge you by whether you are **khon tsai-dii** คนใจดี *a kind-hearted person* and not by your language skills. If you also have excellent Thai language skills, then you have almost become **khon thai** คนไทย, *a Thai person*. You are behaving and speaking as Thai people generally do.

Secret 10

dâai has good manners, and she also respects Thai tradition. **dâai** says: "Be impeccable with your words since your words carry a lot of power."

ได้ มี มารยาท ดี และ เคารพ ประเพณี ของ ไทย – ได้ บอก ว่า – ให้ ใช้ คำ พูด อย่าง ระมัดระวัง เพราะ ว่า คำ พูด ของ คุณ มี พลัง มากๆ

dâai mii maaráyâat dii lɛ́ khauróp pràpheenii khɔ̌ɔng thai – **dâai** bɔ̀ɔk-wâa – hâi tʃái kham-phûut yàang rámátráwang phrɔ́-wâa kham-phûut khɔ̌ɔng khun mii phálang mâak-mâak

dâai have manners good and respect tradition of Thai – **dâai** say that – make use word-speak as cautious because-that word-speak of you have power very-very

dâai ได้ and giving permission

dâai ได้ is commonly used as part of a reply when giving permission to a request.

When giving a positive reply to questions like **dâai-mái** ได้ไหม or **dâai-rú-plàu** ได้ รึ เปล่า, **dâai** ได้ is usually employed with the polite ending particles such as **khá/khráp** คะ/ครับ in order to make a reply sound polite.

A. Sentences with dâai ได้ giving permission

1 Sorry, *may I* stay here?

ขอโทษ นะ คะ – ฉัน อยู่ ที่ นี่ ได้ ไหม
khɔ̌ɔ-thôot ná khá – tʃǎn yùu thîi-nîi *dâai-mái*
sorry ná khâ – I stay place-this *can-question*

Yes, you may stay *anywhere you like*.

ได้ ค่ะ อยู่ ที่ ไหน ก็ ได้
dâai khâ – yùu *thîi-nǎi kɔ̂ɔ-dâai*
can khâ! – stay *place-which also-can*

or simply *Yes*!

ได้ ค่ะ
dâai khâ
can khâ

2 *Can you* help me a little?

ช่วย ฉัน หน่อย ได้ ไหม คะ
tʃûuai tʃǎn nɔ̀i *dâai-mái* khá
help I little *can-question* khá

Yes, certainly!

ได้ อยู่ แล้ว
dâai-yùu-lέεu
can-be-already

or simply *Yes*!

ได้ ค่ะ
dâai khâ
can khâ

3. *Could you* hurry up a little?

รีบ หน่อย ได้ ไหม คะ
rîip nòi *dâai-mái khá*
hurry little *can-question khá*

Yes, for sure!

ได้ เลย ค่ะ
dâai-ləəi khâ
can-sure khâ

or simply *Yes!*

ได้ ค่ะ
dâai khâ
can khâ

B. Highlights

When replying to **dâai-mái** ได้ ไหม questions, the answer usually contains the verb **dâai** ได้.

1. The most simple answer is **dâai khâ** ได้ ค่ะ/ **dâai khráp** ได้ ครับ *yes*.

The polite ending particles **khâ** ค่ะ or **khráp** ครับ are usually necessary with simple replies like this, **dâai khâ** ได้ ค่ะ/ **dâai khráp** ได้ ครับ *yes*.

2. The reply can also be more colourful and informative as follows:

kɔ̂ɔ-dâai ก็ได้ at the end of the sentence is translated as *as you like, it is up to you, anything is fine!*

dâai-yùu-lɛ́ɛu ได้ อยู่ แล้ว is translated into English as *certainly*.

This is a very pleasant expression which can also be understood as *I am already doing it* or *it is already the case*.

dâai-ləəi ได้ เลย *for sure* is a similar expression to **dâai-yùu-lɛ́ɛu** ได้ อยู่ แล้ว *certainly* to say that it is possible for sure. It can be translated into English as *yes, for sure*.

C. Understanding dâai ได้

Generally, **dâai** ได้ can be understood as expressing a positive state of affairs, something that is possible.

In this Secret, we have extended the semantic boundaries of **dâai** ได้ to be used as a part of a reply when giving permission.

The following are common ways to reply to **dâai-mái** ได้ ไหม or **dâai-rʉ́-plàu** ได้ รึ เปล่า questions.

Word order:

> 1. **dâai** + khâ/khráp = *yes*

> 2. kɔ̂ɔ + **dâai** = *showing indifference*
> **kɔ̂ɔ-dâai** = *yes, it is possible, do as you like, it is up to you*

3. **dâai** + yùu-lɛ́ɛu = *showing certainty*
dâai-yùu-lɛ́ɛu = *yes, certainly, for sure!*

4. **dâai** + ləəi = *showing certainty*
dâai-ləəi = *yes, sure, by all means, go ahead!*

Being polite is a built in quality of the Thai language, and **dâai** ได้ plays an important role in this context.

When giving a positive reply to questions like **dâai-mái** ได้ ไหม or **dâai-rú-plàu** ได้ รึ เปล่า, **dâai** ได้ is usually employed with polite ending particles such as **khá/khráp** คะ/ครับ in order to make a reply sound polite.

dâai ได้ can also be used in an idiomatic way with other words in order to give a more colourful reply. **dâai yùu-lɛ́ɛu** ได้ อยู่ แล้ว *yes, certainly, for sure* is a good example.

D. Conclusion

Key: Use **dâai** ได้ as a part of your reply when responding to **dâai-mái** ได้ ไหม questions.

1. In Thai, the question word defines how the reply is formulated. When replying to a **dâai-mái** ได้ ไหม question, **dâai** ได้ is usually included in the reply, **dâai-khâ** ได้ ค่ะ *yes*.

2. **dâai** ได้ is commonly used as a part of a reply when giving permission to a request.

When the question is formulated differently, then a reply is also formulated differently. For example, it is not considered to be good style to reply to **pen-mái** เป็น ไหม *can you* question with **dâai-khâ** ได้ ค่ะ *yes, yes I can.* One should use the word **pen** เป็น in the reply, **pen-khâ** เป็น ค่ะ *yes, yes I can.* See also the following two Secrets 11 and 12 for more information about this.

E. Language hints

> **dâai** ได้ can also be included in the reply when expressing hesitation. We give here a few more examples:

àat-tsà-dâai	อาจ จะ ได้	*maybe, perhaps possible*
nâa-tsà-dâai	น่า จะ ได้	*should be possible*
khong-tsà-dâai	คง จะ ได้	*maybe, might be possible*
hĕn-tsà-dâai	เห็น จะ ได้	*seems, looks likely to be possible*
àat-tsà-mâi-dâai	อาจ จะ ไม่ ได้	*maybe not possible*

Question:

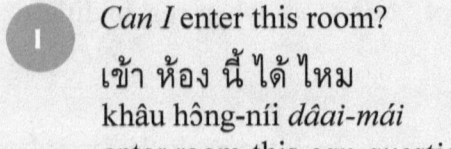

Can I enter this room?
เข้า ห้อง นี้ ได้ ไหม
khâu hông-níi *dâai-mái*
enter room-this *can-question*

Possible answers:

> **1.1** It maybe fine – àat-tsà-dâai อาจ จะ ได้
>
> *It maybe fine* but you need to ask the guard first.
>
> อาจ จะ ได้ แต่ ต้อง ถาม รปภ. ก่อน ครับ
> *àat-tsà-dâai* tɛ̀ɛ tôŋ thǎam rɔɔ pɔɔ phɔɔ kɔ̀ɔn khráp
> *maybe-will-can* but ask guard first khráp

Note that **rɔɔ pɔɔ phɔɔ** รปภ is fully written as follows:

พนัก งาน รักษา ความ ปลอด ภัย
phánák-ngaan ráksǎa kwaam-plɔ̀ɔt-phai
staff care subject-free-danger

Another easier word **yaam** ยาม *guard* is often used instead.

> **1.2** It should be possible – nâa-tsà-dâai น่า จะ ได้
>
> I don't know but it *should be possible*.
>
> ฉัน ไม่ รู้ แต่ น่า จะ ได้ ค่ะ
> tʃǎn mâi rúu tɛ̀ɛ *nâa-tsà-dâai* khâ
> I no know but *should-will-can* khâ

Question:

> **2** *Can I* do it like this?
>
> ทำ แบบ นี้ ได้ ไหม
> tham bɛ̀ɛp-níi *dâai-mái*
> do style-this *can-question*

Possible answers:

> **2.1** Perhaps! – khong-tsà-dâai คง จะ ได้
>
> *Perhaps you can,* but I am not quite sure.
>
> คง จะ ได้ แต่ ผม ไม่ แน่ ใจ ครับ
> *khong-tsà-dâai* tὲε phŏm mâi nêε-tsai khráp
> *perhaps-will-can* but I no certain-heart khráp

Question:

> **3** *Can we* go to watch the car racing *or not?*
>
> ไป ดู รถ แข่ง ได้ รึ เปล่า
> pai duu rót-khὲεng *dâai-rú-plàu*
> go see car-race *can-or-not*

Possible answers:

> **3.1** Not anymore – mâi-dâai lέεu ไม่ ได้ แล้ว
>
> I used to go but now *I can't go anymore.*
>
> ฉัน เคย ไป แต่ ตอน นี้ ไป ไม่ ได้ แล้ว ค่ะ
> tʃǎn khǝǝi pai tὲε tɔɔn-níi pai *mâi-dâai lέεu* khâ
> I used go but at-this go *no-can already* khâ

In the negative reply **mâi** ไม่ *no* is placed before **dâai** ได้.

3.2 It seems that – hĕn-tsà-dâai เห็น จะ ได้

It is a good idea, but *it seems that I can't* go.

เป็น ความ คิด ที่ ดี – แต่ ฉัน เห็น จะ ไป ไม่ ได้ ค่ะ
pen khwaam-khít thîi dii – tὲɛ tʃán *hĕn-tsà* pai *mâi-dâai* khâ
be subject-think that good – but I *see-will* go *no-can* khâ

In the negative reply **mâi** ไม่ *no* is placed before **dâai** ได้.

3.3 Can't because... – mâi-dâai phrɔ́-wâa...ไม่ ได้ เพราะ ว่า...

I can't go because I think it is very dangerous and *I could get* injured.

ไป ไม่ ได้ ค่ะ -เพราะ ว่า – ฉัน คิด ว่า – อันตราย มาก และ อาจ จะ บาด เจ็บ ได้
pai *mâi-dâai* khâ phrɔ́-wâa – tʃán khít wâa – antàraai mâak lé *àat-tsà* bàat-tsèp *dâai*
go *no-can* because-that – I think that – dangerous very and *maybe-will* cut-hurt *can*

In the negative reply **mâi** ไม่ *no* is placed before **dâai** ได้.

F. Simple advice

dâai-yùu-lɛ́ɛu ได้ อยู่ แล้ว *certainly, for sure* or *it is already the case* is a very nice way to express a positive state of affairs. As a language student, concentrate as much as possible on positive expressions. That way you are more easily welcomed into the Thai way of life. **dâai-lɤɤi** ได้ เลย *yes, sure, by all means* is a similar expression and may be used as an alternative.

Learn a few expressions one by one and use them in your daily conversation with your Thai friends.

If you want to express a positive future intention try using **nâa-tsà-dâai** น่า จะ ได้ *should be possible*. In some cases, **àat-tsà-dâai** อาจ จะ ได้ *maybe* in Thai could be understood as a polite way to say *no*.

In the next two Secrets, we shall have a look at how **dâai** ได้ is used in connection with mental and physical actions.

5. dâai ได้ with mental and physical actions

dâai ได้ can be conveniently used as a helping verb to express the possibility of mental or physical actions. Alternatively, we may use either **pen** เป็น or **wăi** ไหว.

Grammatically, **dâai** ได้ behaves in a similar way to **pen** เป็น and **wăi** ไหว. However, the meaning can be different. **pen** เป็น refers *to having skill* only and **wăi** ไหว refers to *having strength* only while **dâai** ได้ can express a range of meanings.

> **Secret 11** dâai ได้ and mental actions
> (dâai lɛ́ kaan kràtham thaang tsai
> ได้ และ การ กระทำ ทาง ใจ)
>
> The meaning is *can, being mentally able to do something.*
>
> **Secret 12** dâai ได้ and physical actions
> (dâai lɛ́ kaan kràtham thaang kaai
> ได้ และ การ กระทำ ทาง กาย)
>
> The meaning is *can, being physically able to do something.*

Secret 11

dâai thinks and speaks only good things. She is very "cool". **dâai** says: "To be yourself and to be able to think independently is your birth right."

ได้ คิด และ พูด แต่ สิ่ง ดีๆ – ได้ เป็น คน ที่ ยอด เยี่ยม มากๆ – ได้ บอก ว่า – การ เป็น ตัว ของ ตัว เอง และ คิด ได้ ด้วย ตัว เอง เป็น สิทธิ์ ของ คุณ ตั้ง แต่ เกิด

dâai khít lɛ́ phûut tɛ̀ɛ dii-dii – **dâai** pen khon thîi yɔ̂ɔt-yîiam mâak-mâak – **dâai** bɔ̀ɔk-wâa – kaan-pen-tuua-khɔ̌ɔng-tuua-eeng lɛ́ khít dâai dûuai tuua-eeng pen sìt khɔ̌ɔng khun tâng-tɛ̀ɛ kə̀ət

dâai think and speak good-good – **dâai** be person top-superb very-very – **dâai** say that – task-be-body-of-body-self and think can by body-self be right of you set-since birth

dâai ได้ and mental actions
(dâai lέ kaan kràtham thaang tsai ได้ และ การ กระทำ ทาง ใจ)

In this Secret, we would like to show how **dâai** ได้ *can* is used in connection with mental activities and how it compares with other similar words like **pen** เป็น *can, knowing how to* and **wăi** ไหว *can, having strength to*.

A. Sentences with dâai ได้, wăi ไหว and pen เป็น referring to mental actions

1 To make – tham ทำ

1.1 To be able to do – tham-dâai ทำ ได้

Some people are talented and *can do* everything.

บาง คน เก่ง และ ทำ ได้ ทุก อย่าง
baang-khon kèng lé *tham-dâai* thúk-yàang
some-person talented and *do-can* every-kind

1.2 To have skill to do – tham-pen ทำ เป็น

Some people are talented and *know how to do* everything.

บาง คน เก่ง และ ทำ เป็น ทุก อย่าง
baang khon kèng lé *tham-pen* thúk-yàang
some-person talented and *do-knowledge* every-kind

1.3 To have strength to do – tham-wăi ทำ ไหว

Some people are strong and *can do* everything.

บาง คน แข็ง แรง และ ทำ ไหว ทุก อย่าง
baang khon khĕng-rεεng lé *tham-wăi* thúk-yàang
some-person strong-power and *do-strength* every-kind

2 To swim – wâai-náam ว่าย น้ำ

2.1 I *can't* swim.

ฉัน ว่าย น้ำ ไม่ ได้
tʃán wâai-náam *mâi-dâai*
I swim-water *no-can*

2.2 I *don't know how* to swim.

ฉัน ว่าย น้ำ ไม่ เป็น
tʃán wâai-náam *mâi-pen*
I swim-water *no-knowledge*

2.3 I *don't have the strength* to swim.

ฉัน ว่าย น้ำ ไม่ ไหว
tʃán wâai-náam *mâi-wǎi*
I swim-water *no-strength*

3 To speak – phûut พูด

3.1 *Can you* speak Japanese?

คุณ พูด ภาษา ญี่ปุ่น ได้ ไหม
khun phûut phaasǎa-yîipùn *dâai-mái*
you speak language-japan *can-question*

3.2 *Do you know how to* speak Japanese?

คุณ พูด ภาษา ญี่ปุ่น เป็น ไหม
khun phûut phaasǎa-yîipùn *pen-mái*
you speak language-japan *knowledge-question*

3.3 *Do you have enough energy* to speak Japanese?
Are you strong enough to speak Japanese?

คุณ พูด ภาษา ญี่ปุ่น ไหว ไหม
khun phûut phaasǎa-yîipùn *wǎi-mái*
you speak language-japan *strength-question*

B. Highlights

Here, we have placed **dâai** ได้ *can, being able to* after the main verb in the same way as in Secret 3. The difference is that in this Secret we are showing how **dâai** ได้ is used in connection with mental activities and how it compares with other similar words such as **pen** เป็น *can, knowing how to* and **wăi** ไหว *can, having strength to*. These two words are used in a more specific way than **dâai** ได้.

> **The summary of the meaning:**
>
> **dâai** ได้ means *can, to be able to* or *to be permitted to do something, whatever the reason.*
>
> **pen** เป็น means *can, to have skill* or *knowledge to do something.*
>
> **wăi** ไหว means *can, to have strength to do something.*

Often the translation into English is the same whether we use **dâai** ได้, **pen** เป็น or **wăi** ไหว in Thai. In Thai, there is a clear difference, however.

Consider the following:

> **1** **tham-dâai thúk-yàang** ทำ ได้ ทุก อย่าง

> **1.1** **baang-khon kèng lé tham-dâai thúk-yàang**
> บาง คน เก่ง และ ทำ ได้ ทุก อย่าง
> *Some people are talented and can do everything.*

tham-dâai ทำ ได้ means *can, being able to do something*. It can also mean *being permitted to* do something. In fact, when **dâai** ได้ is placed at the end of the sentence, it expresses the fact that something can be done *whatever the reason*.

> **1.2 baang khon kèng lɛ́ tham-pen thúk-yàang**
> บาง คน เก่ง และ ทำ เป็น ทุก อย่าง
> *Some people are talented and know how to do everything.*

tham-pen ทำ เป็น means *can, to have mental skill* or *knowledge how to do something* while **tham-dâai** ทำ ได้ *can, to be able to* is used in more general sense.

> **1.3 baang khon khɛ̌ng-rɛɛng lɛ́ tham-wǎi thúk-yàang**
> บาง คน แข็ง แรง และ ทำ ไหว ทุก อย่าง
> *Some people are strong and can do everything.*

Here, we changed the adjective **kèng** เก่ง *talented* to the adjective **khɛ̌ng-rɛɛng** แข็ง แรง *strong* in order to express the true nature of the verb **wǎi** ไหว.

tham-wǎi ทำ ไหว means *can, to have strength to* perform a certain task. **tham-wǎi** ทำ ไหว behaves the same way in the sentence as **tham-dâai** ทำ ได้ and **tham-pen** ทำ เป็น. However, **tham-wǎi** ทำ ไหว refers specifically to having *strength to* do a task while **pen** เป็น refers to *knowledge* and **dâai** ได้ refers to *being able to* or *permitted to*.

The above three phases **tham-dâai** ทำ ได้, **tham-pen** ทำ เป็น and **tham-wǎi** ทำ ไหว could be translated into English as *can do* even though the Thai meaning is different. The difference in meaning is understood from the context in English.

> **2** **wâai-náam mâi-dâai** ว่าย น้ำ ไม่ ได้

> **2.1** **tʃán wâai-náam mâi-dâai**
> ฉัน ว่าย น้ำ ไม่ ได้
> *I cannot swim.*

wâai-náam mâi-dâai ว่าย น้ำ ไม่ ได้ is a negative statement saying that one *cannot, doesn't have the ability to* or *permission to* swim. In fact, swimming is not possible *whatever the reason.*

> **2.2** **tʃán wâai-náam mâi-pen**
> ฉัน ว่าย น้ำ ไม่ เป็น
> *I don't know how to swim.*

This is a simple negative statement with **mâi-pen** ไม่ เป็น *cannot* at the end of the sentence. **mâi-pen** ไม่ เป็น *cannot* refers to the fact that one *doesn't have the skill* or *knowledge* how to swim.

> **2.3** **tʃán wâai-náam mâi-wăi**
> ฉัน ว่าย น้ำ ไม่ ไหว
> *I don't have strength to swim.*

This is a simple negative statement with **mâi-wăi** ไม่ ไหว *cannot* that refers to the fact that one *doesn't have the strength* to perform a task. She is perhaps too tired or weak to do so. **mâi-wăi** ไม่ ไหว is placed at the end of the sentence.

phûut dâai-mái พูด ได้ ไหม

 khun phûut phaasăa-yîipùn dâai-mái
คุณ พูด ภาษา ญี่ปุ่น ได้ ไหม
Can you speak Japanese?

dâai-mái ได้ ไหม *can you* or *are you able to* is placed at the end of the sentence. It refers here to the *ability* to speak a language. Depending on the context, it could also mean *being permitted to speak.*

 khun phûut phaasăa-yîipùn pen-mái
คุณ พูด ภาษา ญี่ปุ่น เป็น ไหม
Do you know how to speak Japanese?

The question **pen-mái** เป็น ไหม *can you, do you know how to* or *do you have skill* or *knowledge,* refers here to the ability to speak the language. It refers to *having skill* only.

khun phûut phaasăa-yîipùn wăi-mái
คุณ พูด ภาษา ญี่ปุ่น ไหว ไหม
Do you know how to speak Japanese?

Similarly, the question **wăi-mái** ไหว ไหม means *can you, do you have strength to* perform the action. **wăi** ไหว refers to *strength* only. Perhaps Japanese is her second language, and she doesn't have the strength to speak it now. It takes too much effort.

C. Understanding dâai ได้

Generally, **dâai** ได้ can be understood as expressing a positive state of affairs, something that is possible.

> **dâai** ได้ as the helping verb after the main verb is often used in connection with mental actions.
>
> In order to understand **dâai** ได้ well, we need to extend its semantic boundaries here to include the *mental ability* to carry out the action. We shall also compare it with **pen** เป็น *to have mental skill* and **wăi** ไหว *to have mental strength*.

One way to understand **dâai** ได้ when it is used as a helping verb, is to take note of whether it stands before or after the main verb. In this Secret **dâai** ได้ is placed after the main verb. The meaning is very different compared to when it is placed before the action verb.

See Secrets 5 and 6 if you wish to review the meaning when **dâai** ได้ is placed directly before the main verb.

Word order:

> 1. subject + verb + object + **dâai** = *mentally able to do something* or *permitted to do something*
>
> kháu + phûut + angkrìt + **dâai** = *He can speak English.*

> 2. subject + verb + object + **pen** = *to have mental skill to do something*
>
> kháu + phûut + angkrìt + **pen** = *He knows how to speak English.*

> 3. subject + verb + object + **wăi** = *to have mental strength to do something*
>
> kháu + phûut + angkrìt + **wăi** = *He has the strength to speak English.*

1. When **dâai** ได้ is placed after the main verb, it is usually placed at the end of the sentence or statement. The grammatical term for this type of an auxiliary or a helping verb is a "modal verb", an example being the English word "can".

   When **dâai** ได้ is used this way, it expresses a range of meanings such as *can, being able to, being permitted to* or *allowed to* do something.

2. Sometimes these three words **dâai** ได้, **pen** เป็น and **wăi** ไหว can be used interchangeably even though the meaning may not be exactly the same.

3. When **dâai** ได้ is placed at the end of the sentence as a helping verb, it expresses a wider range of meanings; the action is possible *whatever the reason* while **pen** เป็น and **wăi** ไหว are more specific. See also the previous Highlights section B.

D. Conclusion

> Key: Place **dâai** ได้ directly after the main verb when the mental action is *possible whatever the reason*. When **dâai** ได้ is placed after the main verb it usually comes at the end of the sentence.

1. **dâai** ได้ has many meanings. That is why it can also be used instead of **pen** เป็น *knowing how to* and **wăi** ไหว *having strength to* in many cases. The exact meaning is then understood from the context. With **dâai** ได้, the action is possible *whatever the reason*.

2. Grammatically, **dâai** ได้ behaves in the same way as **pen** เป็น and **wăi** ไหว. However, the meaning can be different. **pen** เป็น refers to *having skill* only and **wăi** ไหว refers to *having strength* only while **dâai** ได้ can express a range of meanings.

E. Language hints

> **dâai** ได้ as well as **pen** เป็น and **wăi** ไหว are used grammatically in many different ways and have several other meanings depending on the context and how they are used in a sentence.

Consider the following:

A) **dâai** ได้

> **I**
>
> **dâai** ได้ as a main verb *to get*
> To get a bag – **dâai kràpău** ได้ กระเป๋า
>
> Yesterday, I *got* a new bag.
>
> เมื่อ วาน ฉัน ได้ กระเป๋า ใบ ใหม่
> mûːa-waan tʃán *dâai* kràpău bai mài
> yesterday I *get* bag-piece new

dâai kràpău ได้ กระเป๋า *to get a bag*

When **dâai** ได้ as a main verb is placed before a concrete noun, here **kràpău** กระเป๋า, it is translated into English as *to get* or *to receive*.

> **2** dâai ได้ after the main verb
>
> She *can* go out.
>
> เขา ไป เที่ยว ได้
> kháu pai thîiau *dâai*
> she go tour *can*

Here, we use **dâai** ได้ as a helping verb and place it after the action verb. The emphasis is on *can*, *to be able to* or *to have permission to*.

> **3** dâai ได้ before the main verb
>
> She *has already gone* out.
>
> เขา ได้ ไป เที่ยว แล้ว
> kháu *dâai* pai thîiau lɛ́ɛu
> she *get* go tour already

Here, we use **dâai** ได้ as a helping verb and place it before the action verb. The emphasis is on *"getting"* to do something.

> **4** dâai ได้ as a compound verb
> To remember – tsam-dâai จำ ได้
>
> He is already old but still *has a good memory*.
>
> เขา แก่ แล้ว แต่ ยัง จำ ได้ เก่ง มาก
> kháu kɛ̀ɛ lɛ́ɛu tɛ̀ɛ yang *tsam-dâai* kèng mâak
> he old already but still *remember-can* talented very

tsam-dâai จำ ได้ *to remember*

Here, we use **dâai** ได้ as a a compound verb with the prefix **tsam** จำ to express the mental activity, the ability *to remember*. Note that the prefix **tsam** จำ is not usually used alone.

> **5** dâai ได้ before an adjective
>
> I drive a car *well*.
>
> ฉัน ขับ รถ ได้ ดี
> tʃǎn khàp rót *dâai-dii*
> I drive car *can-good*

Here, we use **dâai** ได้ as a kind of prefix and place it before an adjective.

dâai ได้ before an adjective turns it into an adverb, **dâai-dii** ได้ ดี *well*. This statement tells us how well she drives a car.

> **6** dâai ได้ in idiomatic expressions
>
> He *is* really *selfish*.
>
> เขา เอา แต่ ได้ จริงๆ
> kháu *au-tὲɛ-dâai* tsing-tsing
> he *take-but-get* really-really

au-tὲɛ-dâai เอา แต่ ได้ *being selfish*

There are a vast number of idiomatic expressions where **dâai** ได้ is used. See more about idiomatic expressions in Secrets 7 and 8.

B) **pen** เป็น

pen เป็น has several grammatical meanings other than *having skill* or *knowledge how to do* something.

> **1** **pen** เป็น as a main verb – *to be*

> **1.1** He *is* a good person.
>
> เขา เป็น คน ดี
> kháu *pen* khon dii
> he *be* person good

Note that **pen** เป็น cannot usually be placed before an adjective. Here **pen** เป็น *to be* is followed by a noun **khon** คน *person*.

> **1.2** He *is* a good person.
>
> เขา ดี
> kháu dii
> he good

Here, **pen** เป็น is dropped and the classifier **khon** คน *person* can also be dropped.

Adjectives in Thai can play the role of a stative verb. Generally, there are two types of verbs. Stative verbs describe a condition and action verbs describe an action. Here the adjective **dii** ดี *good* is also used as a stative verb, *to be good*.

In spoken Thai, **pen** เป็น *to be* can often be dropped as the main verb in the sentence. Thai people would say simply that **fɛɛn tʃán lɔ̀ɔ** แฟน ฉัน หล่อ *My boyfriend is handsome*.

If **pen** เป็น is used as the main verb followed by an adjective, then we need to use a classifier as well, **fɛɛn tʃán pen khon lɔ̀ɔ** แฟน ฉัน เป็น คน หล่อ *My boyfriend is handsome*.

> Therefore, it is wrong to say, **fɛɛn tʃán pen lɔ̀ɔ** แฟน ฉัน เป็น หล่อ *My boyfriend is handsome*. **pen** เป็น is used as a main verb only before nouns.

> **1.3** This *is* the first time I have tasted durian.
> นี่ เป็น ครั้ง แรก ที่ ฉัน ชิม ทุเรียน
> nîi *pen* khráng-rêɛk thîi tʃǎn tʃim thúriian
> this *be* time-first that I taste durian

Here, **pen** เป็น *to be* is followed by a noun **khráng-rêɛk** ครั้ง แรก *first time*.

> **1.4** I *am* single.
> ผม เป็น โสด
> phǒm *pen* sòot
> I *be* single

pen เป็น as a main verb is not usually followed by an adjective.

With some words, often referring to conditions, such as **sòot** โสด *single*, **pen** เป็น can be followed by an adjective. These are special cases, and one needs to learn them through the usage of the language.

> **2** pen เป็น as a helping verb – *prefix*

> **2.1** He comes here *regularly*.
> เขา มา ที่ นี่ เป็น ประจำ
> kháu maa thîi-nîi *pen-pràtsam*
> he come place-this *be-regular*

pen-pràtsam เป็น ประจำ is translated into English as *regularly*.

pen เป็น is placed here before an adjective **pràtsam** ประจำ *regular, usual*. **pen** เป็น changes an adjective into an adverb.

> **2.2** We will go as a *group*.
>
> เรา จะ ไป เป็น กลุ่ม
> rau tsà pai *pen-klùm*
> we will go *be-group*

Here, the meaning of **pen** เป็น is *as*. It is followed by a noun **klùm** กลุ่ม group.

> **2.3** We will have fun such as chatting with friends and playing games *and so on*.
>
> เรา จะ สนุก กัน – อย่าง เช่น – คุย กับ เพื่อน และ เล่น เกม เป็น ต้น
> rau tsà sànùk kan – yàang tʃên – khui kàp phɯ̂an lέ lên keem *pen-tôn*
> we will fun together – like-example, chat with friend – play game *be-start*

pen-tôn เป็น ต้น is translated into English as *for example* or *and so on*. It is followed by a noun **tôn** ต้น *start*.

> **3** pen เป็น in the compound verb
>
> He is already old but still *must* work hard.
>
> เขา แก่ แล้ว – แต่ ยัง จำ เป็น ต้อง ทำ งาน หนัก
> kháu kὲɛ lέɛu – tὲɛ yang *tsam-pen-tɔ̂ŋ* tham-ngaan nàk
> he old already – but still *must-be-need* do-work heavy

tsam-pen tɔ̂ŋ จำ เป็น ต้อง *have to, must*

The word **tsam** จำ is used as a prefix before the word **pen** เป็น making a meaning *to be compelled to* do something. Here the word **pen** เป็น

is a part of the compound, **tsam-pen** จำ เป็น *have to, must*. We may add the word **tông** ต้อง *must* for more emphasis.

tsam-pen จำ เป็น and **tông** ต้อง have the similar meaning, *must, have to*.

All these three ways have a very similar meaning and the translation into English could be the same *have to, must*, **tsam-pen tông** จำ เป็น ต้อง, **tsam-pen** จำ เป็น and **tông** ต้อง.

> **4** pen เป็น in idiomatic expressions

> **4.1** *What is the matter? What's wrong?*
> เป็น อะไร
> *pen-arai*
> *be what*

Here, **pen** เป็น is used in an idiomatic way. It is followed by a question pronoun **arai** อะไร *what*. The expression **pen-arai** เป็น อะไร is usually translated into English as *What's wrong?* It is often referring to feelings or body conditions.

> **4.2** *Let's conclude that* this is already good enough.
> เอา เป็น ว่า แบบนี้ ดี แล้ว
> *au-pen-wâa* bèɛp-níi dii lɛ́ɛu
> *take-is-that* like-this good already

Usually, the verb **au** เอา *to take, to want* is not followed by a verb. This is, however, an idiomatic expression, and it does not follow the normal grammar rules. Here **au** เอา is followed by the verb **pen** เป็น.

> **5** I *cannot* eat spicy food.
>
> ฉัน กิน อาหาร เผ็ด ไม่ เป็น
> tʃǎn kin aahǎan phèt *mâi-pen*
> I eat food spicy *no-can*

This is a special expression used by Thais to say that *I don't eat spicy food*.

Literally, this expression is translated into English as *I do not have skill to eat spicy food.*

Another way to say the same in English would be *I don't like spicy food* or *it is not my habit to eat spicy food.*

C) *wǎi* ไหว

> **1** Still going strong! – yang wǎi yùu ยัง ไหว อยู่
>
> He is still going *strong*.
>
> เขา ยัง ไหว อยู่
> kháu yang *wǎi* yùu
> he still *strength* stay

This is a short idiomatic expression to say that *he is still going strong*.

> **2** Earthquake
>
> แผ่น ดิน ไหว
> *phèen-din-wǎi*
> sheet-land-shake

One more meaning of **wǎi** ไหว is *to shake, to vibrate,* often used in the connection with **phèen-din-wǎi** แผ่น ดิน ไหว *earthquake*.

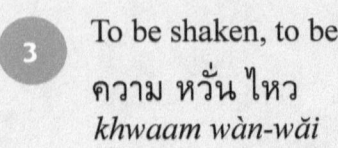

3 To be shaken, to be anxious
ความ หวั่น ไหว
khwaam wàn-wăi
khwaam afraid-shake

This expression **wàn-wăi** หวั่น ไหว refers *to shaking* or *unsteadiness* because of emotion, love, fear etc.

F. Simple advice

When **dâai** ได้ is used as a main verb, it means *to get*. In this Secret we have placed **dâai** ได้ after the main verb as a helping verb to express the mental *ability, being able to* do something.

> If you use **dâai** ได้ instead of **pen** เป็น or **wăi** ไหว, then the exact meaning is understood from the context. With **dâai** ได้ the action *is possible whatever the reason*. It is used in a similar way to the English helping word *can*. More examples when **dâai** ได้ is placed after the action verb are in Secrets 3–4.

pen เป็น behaves in a similar way when expressing the *mental skill to* do something. However, **pen** เป็น is more specific and refers to *mental skill* only. **wăi** ไหว, on the other hand, refers here to *strength* only. In the next Secret 12, we shall review these three verbs when used in the connection with physical activities.

One handy feature of the Thai language is that adjectives can play the role of verbs in the sentence as well, and the main verb can be dropped altogether. **kháu dii** เขา ดี is translated into English as *he is good*.

Secret 12

dâai likes to exercise and take care of herself well.
dâai says: "Eat only food that is good for your health. Don't take too much medicine because it is poison for the body."

ได้ ชอบ ออก กำลังกาย และ ดูแล ตัว เอง เป็น อย่าง ดี – ได้ บอก ว่า – กิน อาหาร ที่ ดี ต่อ สุขภาพ – อย่า กิน ยา มาก เกิน ไป เพราะ ว่า – ยา เป็น พิษ ต่อ ร่าง กาย

dâai tʃɔ̂ɔp ɔ̀ɔk-kamlang-kaai lɛ́ duu-lɛɛ tuua-eeng pen-yàang-dii – **dâai** bɔ̀ɔk-wâa – kin aahăan thîi dii tɔ̀ɔ sùk-khà-phâap – yàa kin yaa mâak kəən-pai phrɔ́-wâa – yaa pen phít tɔ̀ɔ râang-kaai

dâai like produce-power-body and see-look body-self be like good – **dâai** say that – eat food that good for happy-image – don't eat medicine very exceed-go because-that – medicine be poison figure-body

dâai ได้ and physical actions
(dâai lɛ́ kaan kràtham thaang kaai ได้ และ การ กระทำ ทาง กาย)

In this Secret, we will show how **dâai** ได้ is used in connection with physical activities and how it compares with other similar words like **pen** เป็น *can, knowing how to* and **wǎi** ไหว *can, having strength to.*

A. Sentences with dâai ได้, wăi ไหว and pen เป็น referring to physical actions

1 To lift – yók ยก

1.1 This bag is heavy and weighs forty kilograms. *Can* you lift it?

ถุง ใบ นี้ หนัก สี่ สิบ กิโล คุณ ยก ได้ ไหม
thŭng-bai-níi nàk sìi-sìp kìloo – khun yók *dâai-mái*
bag-container-this heavy forty kilogram – you lift *can-question*

1.2 This bag is heavy and weighs forty kilograms. *Do you know how* to lift it?

ถุง ใบ นี้ หนัก สี่ สิบ กิโล – คุณ ยก เป็น ไหม
thŭng-bai-níi nàk sìi-sìp kì-loo – khun yók *pen-mái*
bag-container-this heavy forty kilograms – you lift *knowledge-question*

1.3 This bag is heavy and weighs forty kilograms. *Are you strong enough* to lift it?

ถุง ใบ นี้ หนัก สี่ สิบ กิโล – คุณ ยก ไหว ไหม
thŭng-bai-níi nàk sìi-sìp kì-loo – khun yók *wăi-mái*
bag-container-this heavy forty kilograms – you lift *strength-question*

2 To climb – piin ปีน

2.1 I don't want to go because I *can't* climb mountains.

ฉัน ไม่ อยาก ไป เพราะ ว่า ปีน ภู เขา ไม่ ได้
tʃán mâi-yàak pai phrɔ́-wâa piin phuu-kháu *mâi-dâai*
I no-want go because-that climb mountain-hill *no-can*

2.2 I don't want to go because I *don't know how* to climb mountains.

ฉัน ไม่ อยาก ไป เพราะ ว่า ปีน ภู เขา ไม่ เป็น
tʃán mâi-yàak pai phrɔ́-wâa piin phuu-kháu *mâi-pen*
I no-want go because-that climb mountain-hill *no-knowledge*

2.3 I don't want to go because I *don't have the strength* to climb mountains.

ฉัน ไม่ อยาก ไป เพราะ ว่า ปีน ภู เขา ไม่ ไหว
tʃán mâi-yàak pai phrɔ́-wâa piin phuu-kháu *mâi-wǎi*
I no-want go because-that climb mountain-hill *no-strength*

3 To run – wîng วิ่ง

3.1 He *can* run fast.

เขา วิ่ง เร็วๆ ได้
kháu wîng reu-reu *dâai*
he run fast-fast *can*

3.2 He *knows how* to run fast.

เขา วิ่ง เร็วๆ เป็น
kháu wîng reu-reu *pen*
he run fast-fast *knowledge*

3.3 He *has the strength* to run fast.

เขา วิ่ง เร็วๆ ไหว
kháu wîng reu-reu *wăi*
he run fast-fast *strength*

B. Highlights

Here, we have placed **dâai** ได้ *can, being able to* after the main verb in the same way as in the previous Secret 11 and Secret 3. The difference is that in this Secret we like to demonstrate how **dâai** ได้ is used in connection with physical activities.

dâai ได้ is often used to denote the ability or permission to carry out physical actions in the same way as the English word *can* is used. Usually, we need some special skills, capacity or strength to carry out the task. Sometimes, we also need permission to do the action.

In Thai, we have two other words **pen** เป็น *can* and **wăi** ไหว *can*. They are used in a more specific way compared to **dâai** ได้ when referring to carrying out physical actions.

The difference becomes clear of the following sentences:

> **1.1** **thŭng-bai-níi nàk sìi-sìp kìloo – khun yók dâai-mái**
> ถุง ใบ นี้ หนัก สี่ สิบ กิโล คุณ ยก ได้ ไหม
> *This bag is heavy and weighs forty kilograms. Can you lift it?*

yók dâai-mái ยก ได้ ไหม means *can you* or *are you able to lift?*

yók dâai-mái ยก ได้ ไหม question refers here to the physical act of lifting. It can also be translated into English as *are you allowed* or *permitted to lift?*

> **1.2** **thŭng-bai-níi nàk sìi-sìp kìloo – khun yók pen-mái**
> ถุง ใบ นี้ หนัก สี่ สิบ กิโล คุณ ยก เป็น ไหม
> *This bag is heavy and weighs forty kilograms. Do you know how to lift it?*

yók pen-mái ยก เป็น ไหม question refers here to the mental *ability* or *skill to perform a physical task*. Everyone knows how to lift but it may require certain skills or techniques to lift a heavy bag.

In this context, Thais would most likely prefer to use the term **yók dâai-mái** ยก ได้ ไหม meaning *are you able to lift* or **yók wăi-mái** ยก ไหว ไหม *do you have strength to lift it* instead, since they would think that everybody knows how to lift.

> **1.3** **thŭng-bai-níi nàk sìi-sìp kìloo – khun yók wăi-mái**
> ถุง ใบ นี้ หนัก สี่ สิบ กิโล คุณ ยก ไหว ไหม
> *This bag is heavy and weighs forty kilograms. Are you strong enough to lift it?*

yók wăi-mái ยก ไหว ไหม means *can you, do you have the strength* or *are you strong enough?* **yók wăi-mái** ยก ไหว ไหม is used in a similar way as **yók dâai-mái** ยก ได้ ไหม.

yók wăi-mái ยก ไหว ไหม refers here to the *strength* to carry out a physical task while **yók dâai-mái** ยก ได้ ไหม is used in a more general sense.

> **2.1** tʃán mâi-yàak pai phrɔ́-wâa piin phuu-kháu mâi-dâai
> ฉัน ไม่ อยาก ไป เพราะ ว่า ปีน ภู เขา ไม่ ได้
> *I don't want to go because I can't climb mountains.*

piin mâi-dâai ปีน ไม่ ได้ *cannot climb* can be translated here into English as *I cannot climb, I am not able to climb* or *I am not permitted to climb*. **piin mâi-dâai** ปีน ไม่ ได้ at the end of the sentence refers to the fact that climbing is not possible *whatever the reason*.

> **2.2** tʃán mâi-yàak pai phrɔ́-wâa piin mâi-pen
> ฉัน ไม่ อยาก ไป เพราะ ว่า ปีน ไม่ เป็น
> *I don't want to go because I don't know how to climb.*

piin mâi-pen ปีน ไม่ เป็น *cannot climb* refers here to *not having the mental ability* or *skill to climb*. It may require a certain *skill* or *technique* to climb while **piin mâi-dâai** ปีน ไม่ ได้ *I cannot climb* is used in a more general sense.

> **2.3** tʃán mâi-yàak pai phrɔ́-wâa piin mâi-wăi
> ฉัน ไม่ อยาก ไป เพราะ ว่า ปีน ไม่ ไหว
> *I don't want to go because I don't have the strength to climb.*

piin mâi-wăi ปีน ไม่ ไหว *cannot, not having the strength to climb* can be used in a similar way as **piin mâi-dâai** ปีน ไม่ ได้ *cannot.* **piin**

mâi-dâai ปีน ไม่ ได้ *cannot climb* is used in a more general sense and **piin mâi-pen** ปีน ไม่ เป็น *cannot climb* refers to *not knowing how to*.

> **3.1 kháu wîng reu-reu dâai**
> เขา วิ่ง เร็วๆ ได้
> *He can run fast.*

wîng reu-reu dâai วิ่ง เร็วๆ ได้ refers here to the physical act of running. It can also be translated into English as he *is able* or *is allowed to* run fast. In fact, he can run fast *whatever the reason*.

> **3.2 kháu wîng reu-reu pen**
> เขา วิ่ง เร็วๆ เป็น
> *He knows how to run fast.*

wîng reu-reu pen วิ่ง เร็วๆ เป็น *can, to know how to* or *to have skill* can be used in similar ways to **wîng reu-reu dâai** วิ่ง เร็วๆ ได้ *being able to*.

wîng reu-reu pen วิ่ง เร็วๆ เป็น refers here to having the *ability* or *skill* to run fast. It may require certain *skills* or *techniques* to run fast while **dâai** ได้ *can* is used in a more general sense.

In this context, Thais would most likely prefer to use the term **wîng reu-reu dâai** วิ่ง เร็วๆ ได้ or **wîng reu-reu wăi** วิ่ง เร็วๆ ไหว instead, since they would think that everybody knows how to run.

> **3.3 kháu wîng reu-reu wăi**
> เขา วิ่ง เร็วๆ ไหว
> *He has the strength to run fast.*

wîng reu-reu wăi วิ่ง เร็วๆ ไหว means that he has the *strength* to run fast. **wîng reu-reu wăi** วิ่ง เร็วๆ ไหว refers here to the physical act of running. He can run fast, because he has *enough strength* or *capacity* to perform the action while **wîng reu-reu dâai** วิ่ง เร็วๆ ได้ is used in a more general sense.

C. Understanding dâai ได้

Generally, **dâai** ได้ can be understood as expressing a positive state of affairs, something that is possible.

> **dâai** ได้ can be used as a helping verb after the main verb to refer to *being physically able to* do something.

Word order:

> 1. subject + verb + object + **dâai** = *being physically able* or *allowed to do something*
>
> kháu + wîng + reu-reu + **can** = *He can run fast. He is allowed to run fast.*

> 2. subject + verb + object + **pen** = *to have mental skill to do something*
>
> kháu + wîng + reu-reu + **pen** = *He knows how to run fast.*

> 3. subject + verb + object + **wăi** = *to have strength to do something*
>
> kháu + wîng + reu-reu + **wăi** = *He has stength to run fast.*

dâai ได้ *can* has several meanings when used as a helping verb after the main verb. It can be used for mental and physical activities with meanings *can, being able to*. It can also express *having* or *getting permission to*. Often the exact meaning is understood from the context. In fact, the action is possible *whatever the reason*.

We have two other verbs that are used in a similar way.

wăi ไหว *can, having strength* can be used to refer to *physical* or *mental strength*. Similarly, **pen** เป็น *can, having mental skill* or *knowledge* can be used in connection with physical activities.

One way to understand the deeper meaning of **dâai** ได้ is to use it in a negative sense.

If you use the negative expression **mâi-dâai** ไม่ ได้, then you may be asked a question **tammai** ทำไม *why?* There could be several different reasons.

Examples:

> 1. *I can't climb.*
> ฉัน ปีน ไม่ ได้
> **tʃán piin mâi-dâai**

Now, the question may be asked: **tammai** ทำไม *why?* The reply would start with: **phrɔ́-wâa...** เพราะ ว่า... *because...* There could be many different answers to **tammai** ทำไม *why* question here. For example, because *I do not know how to* or *I don't have the energy to* or *I am not allowed to* or *I have a pain in my legs, I am sick* etc.

> 2. *I do not know how to climb.*
> ฉัน ปีน ไม่ เป็น
> **tʃán piin mâi-pen**

Here, there is only one reason. She doesn't have the skill to perform the action of climbing.

> **3** *I do not have the strength to climb.*
> ฉัน ปีน ไม่ ไหว
> **tʃǎn piin mâi-wǎi**

Here, the reason is that she is tired or she doesn't have the strength to perform the action of climbing.

D. Conclusion

> Key: Place **dâai** ได้ directly after the main verb to express the fact that physical action is possible *whatever the reason.*

1. Alternatively, you may place either **pen** เป็น or **wǎi** ไหว after the main verb to express specific meanings like *knowing how to* or *having strength to.*

2. On many occasions, **dâai** ได้ may be used instead of **wǎi** ไหว or **pen** เป็น. Then the specific meaning is understood from the context. However, when one wants to emphasize the physical or mental aspect of *having strength*, then **wǎi** ไหว is a better choice or when one wants to express the *mental skill*, then **pen** เป็น is a better choice.

3. In order to understand **dâai** ได้ well, we need to extend its semantic boundaries to include *ability* or *capacity* to carry out physical actions whatever the reason. In this context, **wǎi** ไหว and **pen** เป็น behave grammatically in the same way as **dâai** ได้.

4. Just make sure that you use these words correctly when replying to a question. In Thai, a part of the question is repeated in the reply. In English it is usually enough to say *yes* or *no*.

Examples:

A Question with **dâai** ได้
yók-dâai-mái ยก ได้ ไหม *Can you lift it?*

Positive reply: **yók-dâai** ยก ได้ *Yes, I can.*

Negative reply: **yók-mâi-dâai** ยก ไม่ ได้
No, I cannot. / I am not able to.

B Question with **pen** เป็น
yók-pen-mái ยก เป็น ไหม
Can you lift it, do you have the skill to lift it?

Positive reply: **yók-pen** ยก เป็น
Yes, I can. / I know how to.

Negative reply: **yók-mâi-pen** ยก ไม่ เป็น
No, I cannot. / I do not know how to.

C Question with **wăi** ไหว
yók-wăi-mái ยก ไหว ไหม
Can you lift it, are you strong enough to lift it?

Positive reply: **yók-wăi** ยก ไหว
Yes, I can. / Yes, I am strong enough.

Negative reply: **yók-mâi-wăi** ยก ไม่ ไหว
No, I cannot. / I am not strong enough.

E. Language hints

> We shall review here, once more, the three important helping verbs that can be used grammatically in the same way, but they express somewhat different meanings. They are **dâai** ได้, **wăi** ไหว and **pen** เป็น.

These three verbs can be used in connection with either mental or physical actions. See also Secret 11 for mental actions.

The meaning in English is as follows:

dâai	ได้	can, being able to, having permission to
pen	เป็น	can, having the skill, knowing how to
wăi	ไหว	can, having the strength to

In order to understand the difference clearly, consider the following:

1 Swimming:
- dâai ได้
- pen เป็น
- wăi ไหว

1.1 He *can* swim.
เขา ว่าย น้ำ ได้
kháu wâai-náam *dâai*
he swim-water *can*

dâai ได้ can refer to physical or mental activity.

Depending on the context, the verb **dâai** ได้ could be translated here into English in several ways: *he can swim, he is able to swim, he has* *permission to swim* or *he is allowed to swim*. The action is possible whatever the reason.

> **1.2** He *knows how* to swim.
> เขา ว่าย น้ำ เป็น
> kháu wâai-náam *pen*
> he swim-water *knowledge*

pen เป็น refers usually to the *mental skill* only.

pen เป็น means *having the skill, ability* or *knowledge how* to swim.
pen เป็น is used here to express the mental skill to perform the physical activity.

> **1.3** I *have no strength* to swim.
> ฉัน ว่าย น้ำ ไม่ ไหว
> tʃǎn wâai-náam *mâi wǎi*
> I swim-water *no-strength*

Here, **mâi-wǎi** ไม่ ไหว refers to the fact that *she has no strength to swim*.

wǎi ไหว *can, to have strength* is used here to express either *physical* or *mental strength*.

> **2** Not being able to eat spicy food:
> • mâi-dâai ไม่ ได้
> • mâi-pen ไม่ เป็น
> • mâi-wǎi ไม่ ไหว

> **2.1** I *can't* eat spicy food.
> กิน อาหาร เผ็ด ไม่ ได้
> kin aahăan phèt *mâi-dâai*
> eat food spicy *no-can*

dâai ได้ can refer to physical or mental activity.

Here, **mâi-dâai** ไม่ ได้ *cannot, not being able to, not having permission to* or *not being allowed to* is used to express the fact that he can't eat spicy food *whatever the reason*.

> **2.2** I *don't* eat spicy food.
> กิน อาหาร เผ็ด ไม่ เป็น
> kin aahăan phèt *mâi-pen*
> eat food spicy *no-knowledge*

pen เป็น refers usually to the mental skill only.

When referring to eating and drinking the meaning of **pen** เป็น can be somewhat different than when it is used with other common verbs. The literal translation of **pen** เป็น here is *I don't know how to eat spicy food.*

As Westerners, we would think that everyone knows how to eat spicy food even though he may not like it. Since we don't use a similar expression in English, the more correct translation into English would be *I don't eat spicy food* or *I am not accustomed to eat spicy food* or *spicy food is not a part of my diet.*

> **2.3** I *have no strength* to eat spicy food.
>
> กิน อาหาร เผ็ด ไม่ ไหว
> kin aahăan phèt *mâi-wăi*
> eat food spicy *no-strength*

wăi ไหว can refer to physical and also mental *strength.*

mâi-wăi ไม่ ไหว means *cannot, not having strength.* Here **mâi-wăi** ไม่ ไหว means that *he has no strength to eat spicy food.* It takes too much effort to do so.

> **3** He can run fast:
> - dâai ได้
> - wăi ไหว
> - pen เป็น

> **3.1** He is already old but still *able* to run fast.
>
> เขา แก่ แล้ว แต่ ยัง วิ่ง ได้ เร็ว อยู่
> kháu kèe léɛu tɛ̀ɛ yang wîng *dâai* reu yùu
> he old already but still run *can* fast stay

dâai ได้ can refer to physical or mental activity.

Here, **dâai** ได้ *can, being able to* or *having permission* to is used to express the *physical* activity. He is able to run fast *whatever the reason.*

> **3.2** He is already old but still *knows how* to run fast.
>
> เขา แก่ แล้ว แต่ ยัง วิ่ง เร็ว เป็น อยู่
> kháu kèe léɛu tɛ̀ɛ yang wîng reu *pen* yùu
> he old already but still run fast *knowledge* stay

pen เป็น refers usually to the mental skill only while referring to mental or physical activities.

This sentence is grammatically correct but it sounds odd in Thai. **pen** เป็น is strongly associated with mental skills, and Thais think that everyone knows how to run, they would perhaps use here **dâai** ได้ or **wăi** ไหว instead.

> **3.3** He is already old but still *able* to run fast.
> เขา แก่ แล้ว แต่ ยัง วิ่ง เร็ว ไหว อยู่
> kháu kèe lɛ́ɛu tɛ̀ɛ yang wîng reu *wăi* yùu
> he old already but still run *strength* stay

wăi ไหว can refer to physical or mental *strength*.

wăi ไหว *can, having strength* expresses the physical or mental strength. Here, **wăi** ไหว refers to physical strength.

> **4** There is one more word in Thai that is used to express *to have skills* with a similar meaning to **pen** เป็น. That is the noun **fĭi-muu** ฝี มือ *skill, ability, craftsmanship*.

While **dâai** ได้, **pen** เป็น and **wăi** ไหว are verbs, **fĭi muu** ฝี มือ is a noun.

fĭi muu ฝี มือ is mainly used as special skill or ability referring to actions performed by hand, *craftsmanship*.

> **4.1** To have photography *skill*.
> ฝี มือ ถ่าย รูป
> *fĭi muu* thàai rûup
> *skill* take-picture

4.2 To have acting *skills*.

ฝี มือ การ แสดง
fĭi muu kaan-sàdɛɛng
skill task-act

4.3 He is *a skilful craftsman*.

เขา มี ฝี มือ
kháu mii *fĭi muu*
he have *skill*

F. Simple advice

In Thai, we use three different words which can be translated into English as *can*, namely **dâai** ได้, **pen** เป็น and **wăi** ไหว.

It is fine if you first learn to use properly the helping verb **dâai** ได้ *can, being able to* or *being allowed to* carry out mental or physical activities since it can be used in most cases; it is used in the same way as the English word *can*.

If you want to express yourself more precisely in some specific situations, then **pen** เป็น *having mental skill* or **wăi** ไหว *having physical* or *mental strength* may be used.

6. dâai ได้ and negative actions
(dâai lɛ́ pràyòok pàtìsèet ได้ และ ประโยค ปฏิเสธ)

mâi-dâai ไม่ ได้ *cannot* can be placed after or before the main verb; the meaning is very different.

mâi-dâai ไม่ ได้ after the main verb means *cannot, not being able to, not being allowed to* or *not having permission to*. It is often used instead of **mâi-pen** ไม่ เป็น *cannot, not having skill to* or **mâi-wăi** ไม่ ไหว *cannot, not having strength to*.

When **mâi-dâai** ไม่ ได้ is placed before the action verb, it often refers to past time action. The meaning in English is *did not* or *did not get an opportunity to*. Depending on the context, **mâi-dâai** ไม่ ได้ can also refer to the present time or even to the future time actions.

> **Secret 13** **mâi-dâai** ไม่ ได้ after the main verb
> (mâi-dâai lăng krì-yaa làk ไม่ ได้ หลัง กริยา หลัก)
>
> The meaning is *cannot, not being allowed to, not having permission to.*
>
> **Secret 14** mâi-dâai ไม่ ได้ before the main verb
> (mâi-dâai kɔ̀ɔn krìyaa làk ไม่ ได้ ก่อน กริยา หลัก)
>
> The meaning is *did not, do not, did not get an opportunity to.*

Secret 13

dâai likes many things. **dâai** says: "Don't make assumptions. Try something before you make up your mind and see if it is possible."

ได้ ชอบ เรื่อง หลาย เรื่อง – ได้ บอก ว่า – อย่า คาด เดา อะไร ล่วง หน้า ลอง ดู ก่อน – ที่ จะ ตัด สิน ใจ ว่า ได้ หรือ ไม่ ได้

dâai tʃɔ́ɔp rûuang lăai rûuang – **dâai** bɔ̀ɔk-wâa – yàa khâat-dau arai lûuang-nâa – lɔɔng-duu kɔ̀ɔn – thîi tsà tàt-sĭn-tsai wâa dâai rŭu mâi-dâai

dâai like thing several thing – dâai say that – don't expect-anticipate what ahead-next – try-see first – that will decide that can or no-can

dâai ได้ and negative sentences – **mâi-dâai** ไม่ ได้ after the main verb
(dâai lɛ́ pràyòok pàtisèet ได้ และ ประโยค ปฏิเสธ)

Depending on the context **mâi-dâai** ไม่ ได้ after the main verb means *cannot, not being able to, not being permitted to* or *not being allowed to.*

A. Sentences with mâi-dâai ไม่ ได้ mâi-pen ไม่ เป็น and mâi-wăi ไม่ ไหว when placed after the action verb

1 Speaking Chinese – phûut phaasăa tsiin
พูด ภาษา จีน

1.1 He *can't* speak Chinese.

เขา พูด ภาษา จีน ไม่ ได้
kháu phûut phaasăa tsiin *mâi-dâai*
he speak language-China *no-can*

1.2 He *doesn't know how* to speak Chinese.

เขา พูด ภาษา จีน ไม่ เป็น
kháu phûut phaasăa tsiin *mâi-pen*
he speak language-china *no-knowledge*

1.3 He doesn't *have the strength* to speak Chinese.

เขา พูด ภาษา จีน ไม่ ไหว
kháu phûut phaasăa tsiin *mâi-wăi*
he speak language-china *no-strength*

2 Making delicious food – tham aahăan arɔ̀ɔi-arɔ̀ɔi
ทำ อาหาร อร่อยๆ

2.1 I *can't* make delicious food.

ฉัน ทำ อาหาร อร่อยๆ ไม่ ได้
tʃán tham aahăan arɔ̀ɔi-arɔ̀ɔi *mâi-dâai*
I do food delicious *no-can*

2.2 I *don't know how* to make delicious food.

ฉัน ทำ อาหาร อร่อยๆ ไม่ เป็น
tʃán tham aahăan arɔ̀ɔi-arɔ̀ɔi *mâi-pen*
I do food delicious *no-knowledge*

2.3 I *don't have the strength* to make delicious food.

ฉัน ทำ อาหาร อร่อยๆ ไม่ ไหว
tʃán tham aahăan arɔ̀ɔi-arɔ̀ɔi *mâi-wăi*
I do food delicious *no-strength*

3 Going far – pai klai ไป ไกล

3.1 It is too far, I *can't* go.

มัน ไกล เกิน ไป – ไป ไม่ ได้
man klai kəən-pai – pai *mâi-dâai*
it far exceed-go – go *no-can*

3.2 It is too far, I *don't know how* to get there.

มัน ไกล เกิน ไป – ไป ไม่ เป็น
man klai kəən-pai – pai *mâi-pen*
it far exceed-go – go *no-knowledge*

3.3 It is too far, I *have no strength* to go.

มัน ไกล เกิน ไป – ไป ไม่ ไหว
man klai kəən-pai – pai *mâi-wăi*
it far exceed-go – go *no-strength*

B. Highlights

Here, we have placed **mâi-dâai** ไม่ ได้ after the main verb. It can have several different meanings like *cannot, not being able to, not being permitted to* or *not being allowed to*. The context would reveal the correct meaning. In fact, the action is not possible *whatever the reason*.

Two other phrases **mâi-pen** ไม่ เป็น *not having skill* or *ability to* do something and **mâi-wăi** ไม่ ไหว *not having strength to* do something are used grammatically in the same way as **mâi-dâai** ไม่ ได้ *cannot*.

Consider the following:

>  **kháu phûut phaasăa tsiin mâi-dâai**
> เขา พูด ภาษา จีน ไม่ ได้
> *He cannot speak Chinese.*

phûut mâi-dâai พูด ไม่ ได้ is used here to express the mental ability, *not being able to* speak. In some context, this statement can also be translated into English as *not being allowed to*. In fact, he cannot speak Chinese *whatever the reason*.

> **kháu phûut phaasăa tsiin mâi-pen**
> เขา พูด ภาษา จีน ไม่ เป็น
> *He does not know how to speak Chinese.*

The meaning of **phûut mâi-pen** พูด ไม่ เป็น is limited to *not having knowledge* or *skill to* speak. He cannot speak Chinese because he *does not know how to*.

> **kháu phûut phaasăa tsiin mâi-wăi**
> เขา พูด ภาษา จีน ไม่ ไหว
> *He does not have strength to speak Chinese.*

phûut mâi-wăi พูด ไม่ ไหว is used grammatically in a similar way as **mâi-dâai** ไม่ ได้ *cannot* and **mâi-pen** ไม่ เป็น *not having skill to*. **mâi-wăi** ไม่ ไหว means here *not having strength* physically or mentally to speak Chinese.

Perhaps, he knows Chinese but he won't speak it now since he has *no strength*. His knowledge of Chinese is perhaps limited and it takes too much effort to do so.

tʃán tham aahăan arɔ̀ɔi-arɔ̀ɔi mâi-dâai
ฉัน ทำ อาหาร อร่อยๆ ไม่ ได้
I cannot make delicious food.

tham mâi-dâai ทำ ไม่ ได้ is used here to express the ability, *not being able to* make delicious food. In fact, she cannot make delicious food *whatever the reason*.

Perhaps, she *does not know how to*. Maybe, she has *no place* to do so. It could also be that making delicious food is *too expensive* or she *is not being allowed to* etc.

tʃán tham aahăan arɔ̀ɔi-arɔ̀ɔi mâi-pen
ฉัน ทำ อาหาร อร่อยๆ ไม่ เป็น
I don't know how to make delicious food.

tham mâi-pen ทำ ไม่ เป็น is used here to express the mental ability, *not having knowledge how to* make delicious food. The reason she cannot make delicious food is because she has *no skill*, she *doesn't know how to*.

tʃán tham arɔ̀ɔi-arɔ̀ɔi mâi-wăi
ฉัน ทำ อาหาร อร่อยๆ ไม่ ไหว
I don't have the strength to make delicious food.

tham mâi-wăi ทำ ไม่ ไหว means that she cannot make delicious food because it takes *too much effort* to do so, she *has no strength*. Perhaps she is able to and knows how to but now she is *too tired* or *not in the mood*.

mâi-wăi ไม่ ไหว *cannot* is used grammatically in a similar way as **mâi-dâai** ไม่ ได้ *cannot* and **mâi-pen** ไม่ เป็น *not having skill* or *ability*.

man klai kəən-pai – pai mâi-dâai
มัน ไกล เกิน ไป – ไป ไม่ ได้
It is too far, I can't go.

pai mâi-dâai ไป ไม่ ได้ is used here to express the ability, *not being able to* go. In fact, she cannot go *whatever the reason*. Perhaps, she *does not want to* go. Maybe, it is *too expensive* or *she is not being allowed to* etc.

Here, we have translated **mâi-dâai** ไม่ ได้ into English as *cannot*. The exact meaning is understood from the context.

man klai kəən-pai – pai mâi-pen
มัน ไกล เกิน เกิน ไป – ไป ไม่ เป็น
It is too far, I don't know how to get there.

The meaning of **pai mâi-pen** ไป ไม่ เป็น is limited here to *not knowing a way*. She cannot go there because she *hasn't got the knowledge* of how to get there. The way is unknown to her.

However, since the verb **pen** ไป is so strongly associated with having skill, Thais would perhaps in this context use another expression like:

> **man klai kəən-pai – pai mâi-thùuk**
> มัน ไกล เกิน ไป – ไป ไม่ ถูก
> *It is too far. I don't know how to get there.*

or

> **man klai kəən-pai – mâi rúu tsà pai yang-ngai**
> มัน ไกล เกิน ไป – ไม่ รู้ จะ ไป ยัง ไง
> *It is too far. I don't know how to get there.*

3.3 man klai kɔɔn-pai pai mâi-wăi
มัน ไกล เกิน ไป – ไป ไม่ ไหว
It is too far, I have no strength to go.

pai mâi-wăi ไป ไม่ ไหว is used grammatically the same way as **pai mâi-dâai** ไป ไม่ ได้ and **pai mâi-pen** ไป ไม่ เป็น. Its meaning is limited to *not having strength to go*. Perhaps she is too tired, mentally or physically, to go.

C. Understanding mâi-dâai ไม่ ได้

Generally, **mâi-dâai** ไม่ ได้ can be understood as *cannot*. The action is *not possible* or *cannot be done*.

In order to understand **mâi-dâai** ไม่ ได้ *cannot* well, we need to extend its semantic boundaries to include the negative actions, denial of carrying out the action *whatever the reason*.

mâi-dâai ไม่ ได้ at the end of the statement meaning *cannot, not being able to, not being allowed to* or *not having permission to* is often used instead of **mâi-pen** ไม่ เป็น *cannot, not having skill to* or **mâi-wăi** ไม่ ไหว *cannot, not having strength to*.

mâi-dâai ไม่ ได้ *cannot*, when placed after the main verb, comes usually at the end of the sentence. It can have different meanings. It can express *mental* or *physical* ability, *not being able to* do something. In addition, it is used to express *not having permission* or *not being allowed to* do something. The action is not possible *whatever the reason*.

Word order:

> subject + verb + object + **mâi-dâai** = *cannot, not being able to, not being allowed to*
>
> tʃán + tham + **mâi-dâai** = *I cannot do it.*

Depending on the context the following simple Thai statement can express several different meanings in English:

> ทำ ไม่ ได้
> tham *mâi-dâai*
> do *no-can*

1. It is impossible to do the action – It can't be done!
   mâi-dâai ไม่ ได้ *cannot* is used here to express the impossibility of carrying out the action whatever the reason.

2. Not being able to – I (he, she, we, they, John etc.) can't do it.
   mâi-dâai ไม่ ได้ *cannot* can be used to express the physical or mental ability of not being able to do something.

3. Not being allowed to – I am not allowed to do it.
   mâi-dâai ไม่ ได้ *cannot* can be used to express not having permission or not being allowed to do something.

4. Not having skill to – I don't know how to do it.
   Instead of **mâi-dâai** ไม่ ได้ *cannot*, we could use the phrase **mâi-pen** ไม่ เป็น, *not having skill*.

   mâi-pen ไม่ เป็น cannot can only be used to express not having the mental skill to do something.

5. Not having strength to – I don't have the strength to do it.
   Instead of **mâi-dâai** ไม่ ได้ *cannot* we could use the phrase **mâi-wăi** ไม่ ไหว.

mâi-wăi ไม่ ไหว *cannot* can be used to express the mental or physical strength to do something.

In all of the above five cases, we could use the phrase **mâi-dâai** ไม่ ได้ that is translated into English as *cannot*. Then the correct meaning must be understood from the context or from the additional information which may be available.

D. Conclusion

> Key: Place **mâi-dâai** ไม่ ได้ *cannot* after the main verb to express the fact that the action is not possible *whatever the reason*.

1. **mâi-dâai** ไม่ ได้, at the end of the statement, can express English meanings like *cannot, not possible, not being able to* or *not being allowed to* do something.

2. The main verb can refer either to mental or physical activity. We have deliberately chosen the two other similar verbs for comparison since that will help you to understand **mâi-dâai** ไม่ ได้ better.

3. All the following verb constructions are used grammatically in the same way but can have different meanings.

   mâi-dâai ไม่ ได้ *cannot, not being able to* or *not having permission to, the action is not possible whatever the reason*

   mâi-pen ไม่ เป็น *not having the skill to, not knowing how to*

   mâi-wăi ไม่ ไหว *not having the strength to*

4. **mâi-dâai** ไม่ ได้ may in many cases be used instead of **mâi-pen** ไม่ เป็น or **mâi-wăi** ไม่ ไหว. Then, the exact meaning is understood from the context.

E. Language hints

We give here more examples of **mâi-dâai** ไม่ ได้, **mâi-pen** ไม่ เป็น and **mâi-wăi** ไม่ ไหว when placed after the main verb.

These three expressions **mâi-dâai** ไม่ ได้, **mâi-pen** ไม่ เป็น and **mâi-wăi** ไม่ ไหว behave in negative sentences and after the main verb in a similar way as they behave in positive statements.

A) **mâi-dâai** ไม่ ได้ after the main verb

> **1** Not being allowed to – mâi-dâai ไม่ ได้

>> **1.1** You *can't* stay here.
>> อยู่ ที่ นี่ ไม่ ได้
>> yùu thîi-nîi *mâi-dâai*
>> stay place-this *no-can*

mâi-dâai ไม่ ได้ *cannot, not allowed to, not having permission to*

Here, **mâi-dâai** ไม่ ได้ *cannot* is used in the sense of *not having permission* or *not being allowed to* do something. The permission is not granted whatever the reason.

>> **1.2** At school he *can't* speak Isaan.
>> ที่ โรงเรียน เขา พูด ภาษา อีสาน ไม่ ได้
>> thîi roong-riian kháu phûut phaasăa-iisăan *mâi-dâai*
>> at school he speak language-Isaan *no-can*

mâi-dâai ไม่ ได้ *cannot* can be used to express *not having permission* or *not being allowed to* do something. The reason he can't speak Isaan at school is because it is *not allowed*. Everyone must learn to speak Thai.

> **1.3** Not allowing – mâi-anúyâat-hâi ไม่ อนุญาต ให้
>
> He *does not allow* me to stay here.
>
> เขา ไม่ อนุญาต ให้ อยู่ ที่ นี่
> kháu *mâi-anúyâat-hâi* yùu thîi-nîi
> he *no-let-allow* stay place-this

This is a similar meaning with **mâi-anúyâat-hâi** ไม่ อนุญาต ให้.

mâi-anúyâat-hâi ไม่ อนุญาต ให้ means *not giving permission* while **mâi-dâai** ไม่ ได้ means *not getting permission*.

> **2** Not being able to – mâi-dâai ไม่ ได้

> **2.1** That mountain is very steep. You won't be able to climb it!
>
> ภู เขา ลูก นั้น สูง ชัน มาก – ปีน ไม่ ได้
> phuu-kháu lûuk nán sǔung-tʃan mâak – piin *mâi-dâai*
> mountain-hill classifier that high-steep very – climb *no-can*

mâi-dâai ไม่ ได้ *cannot* can be used to express the *impossibility of carrying out the action* either mentally or physically. **lûuk** ลูก is a classifier used for mountains and hills.

> **2.2** This work is too heavy, I am *not able* to do it at all.
>
> งาน นี้ หนัก เกิน ไป – ทำ ไม่ ได้ หรอก
> ngaan níi nàk kəən-pai – tham *mâi-dâai* rɔ̀ɔk
> work this heavy exceed-go – *do no-can* rɔ̀ɔk

mâi-dâai ไม่ ได้ *cannot, not being able to.*

Here, **mâi-dâai** ไม่ ได้ *cannot* is used to express the *physical ability not being able physically to do* that work. The exact meaning is understood from the context.

rɔ̀ɔk หรอก is a particle that is used in negative sentences in order to place more emphasis on the statement. It is not easy to translate into English. The best translation here is probably *at all*.

> **3** Cannot be done – mâi-dâai ไม่ ได้

> **3.1** This work *can't be* done.
>
> งาน นี้ ทำ ไม่ ได้
> ngaan-níi tham *mâi-dâai*
> work-this do *no-can*

mâi-dâai ไม่ ได้ *cannot* can be used to express the impossibility of carrying out the action *whatever the reason.*

B) **mâi-pen** ไม่ เป็น and **mâi-wăi** ไม่ ไหว after the main verb

> **1**
> He *does not know how* to speak Isaan.
>
> เขา พูด ภาษา อีสาน ไม่ เป็น
> kháu phûut phaasǎa iisǎan *mâi-pen*
> he speak language-Isaan *no-knowledge*

mâi-pen ไม่ เป็น *cannot* can be used to express *not having knowledge* or *ability to* do something. The reason he can't speak Isaan is because he has no knowledge of that language.

> **2**
> He *has no strength* to speak Chinese.
>
> เขา พูด ภาษา จีน ไม่ ไหว
> kháu phûut phaasǎa tsiin *mâi-wǎi*
> he speak language-China *no-strength*

In this sentence **mâi-wǎi** ไม่ ไหว means that he *lacks the strength* to speak Chinese. Perhaps, it is too difficult.

> **3**
> It is too far. I *have no strength* to walk.
>
> ไกล เกิน ไป เดิน ไป ไม่ ไหว
> klai kəən pai dəən-pai *mâi-wǎi*
> far exceed-go walk *no-strength*

wǎi ไหว is expressing physical or mental strength.

In this sentence **mâi-wǎi** ไม่ ไหว means that he lacks the *physical* or *mental strength* to walk that far.

> **C)** When replying to the question the same question word is usually repeated in the reply.

Consider the following:

Question: *Can* you speak Japanese?

คุณ พูด ภาษา ญี่ปุ่น ได้ ไหม คะ
khun phûut phaa-săa yîipùn *dâai-mái* khá
you speak language Japan *can-question* khá

Positive reply:
Yes, I *can*. (I am able)
ได้ ค่ะ
dâai khâ
can khâ

Negative reply:
No, I *can't*. (I am not able)
ไม่ ได้ ค่ะ
mâi-dâai khâ
no-can khâ

Question: *Can* you speak Lao?

คุณ พูด ภาษา ลาว เป็น ไหม ครับ
khun phûut phaasăa laau *pen-mái* khráp
you speak language-Lao *knowledge-question* khráp

Positive reply:
Yes, I *can*.
(I have the knowledge)
เป็น ครับ
pen khráp
have knowledge khráp

Negative reply:
No, I *can't*.
(I don't have the knowledge)
ไม่ เป็น ครับ
mâi-pen khráp
no-knowledge khráp

Note that it is not good style to reply to **pen-mái** เป็น ไหม question as **dâai khráp** ได้ ครับ.

Question: Can you do it? (Do you have the strength?)

ทำ ไหว ไหม
tham *wăi-mái*
do *strength-question*

Positive reply:
Yes, I *can*.
(I have the strength)
ทำ ไหว ค่ะ
tham *wăi khâ*
do *no-strength khâ*

Negative reply:
No, I *can't*.
(I don't have the strength)
ทำ ไม่ ไหว ค่ะ
tham *mâi-wăi khâ*
do *no-strength khâ*

F. Simple advice

One particular feature of using negative statements in Thai is to learn to say them in a positive way. To be humble is the key. It is good to make negative statements sound more positive in which ever way you can. The way you say it and the words you choose to use are important.

In Thai, you should respect everyone and be polite regardless of their position or status. This is true in every country, but in Thailand being polite is built into the language more than in many other languages.

Therefore, it is important to use polite request particles like **khâ** ค่ะ and **khráp** ครับ in negative replies, **mâi-dâai khâ/khráp** ไม่ ได้ ค่ะ/ครับ.

> One interesting fact is that **mâi-dâai** ไม่ได้ can be placed *before* and *after* the main verb while **mâi-pen** ไม่เป็น and **mâi-wăi** ไม่ไหว are usually only placed *after* the main verb.

In the next Secret 14, we shall demonstrate the meaning of **mâi-dâai** ไม่ได้ when placed before the main verb. The meaning and the usage is quite different to when it is placed after the main verb.

Secret 14

dâai is a sophisticated person. It is not very easy to understand how she really is. **dâai** says: "Life has many faces. It changes every day and is never the same."

ได้ เป็น คน หรู หรา – เรา ไม่ สามารถ เข้า ใจ ได้ ง่ายๆ ว่า เขา เป็น ยัง ไง – ได้ บอก ว่า – ชีวิต มี รสชาติ หลาย แบบ – มัน เปลี่ยนไป ทุก วัน และ ทุก ครั้ง ก็ ไม่ เหมือน กัน

dâai pen khon rŭu-răa – rau mâi săa-mâat khâu-tsai dâai ngâai-ngâai wâa kháu pen-yang-ngai – **dâai** bɔ̀ɔk wâa – tʃiiwít mii rót-tʃâat lăai bɛ̀ɛp – man pliian pai thúk-wan lɛ́ thúk-khráng kɔ̂ɔ mâi mŭɯan-kan

dâai be person elegant-highly – we no able enter-heart can easy-easy that she be-how – **dâai** say that – life have flavour-nature many kind – every-day every-time no like-each-other

dâai ได้ and negative sentences – mâi-dâai ไม่ได้ before the main verb

When **mâi-dâai** ไม่ได้ is placed before the action verb, it often refers to a past time action. The meaning in English is *did not* or *did not get an opportunity to*. Depending on the context, **mâi-dâai** ไม่ได้ can also refer to the present time or even to future time actions.

A. Sentences with mâi-dâai ไม่ ได้ before the main verb

1 Happening now or nowadays

1.1 Nowadays, I *don't* go to school.

เดี๋ยว นี้ ฉัน ไม่ ได้ ไป โรง เรียน
dǐiau-níi tʃǎn *mâi-dâai* pai roong-riian
moment-this I *no-get* go building-study

1.2 Nowadays, I *don't* eat at night-time any more.

ตอน นี้ ฉัน ไม่ ได้ กิน ข้าว ตอน กลาง คืน แล้ว
tɔɔn-níi tʃǎn *mâi-dâai* kin khâau tɔɔn klaang-khɯɯn lɛ́ɛu
at-this I *no-get* eat rice at middle-night already

2 Happened in the past

2.1 Yesterday, *I didn't* do anything.

เมื่อวาน ฉัน ไม่ ได้ ทำ อะไร
mɯ̂ɯa-waan tʃǎn *mâi-dâai* tham arai
yesterday I *no-get* do what

2.2 I *didn't* wear shoes in the room.

ฉัน ไม่ ได้ ใส่ รอง เท้า ใน ห้อง
tʃǎn *mâi-dâai* sài rɔɔng-tháu nai hɔ̂ng
I *no-get* wear carry-foot in room

3 Will not happen in the future

3.1 Tomorrow, I *am not going* out.

พรุ่ง นี้ ฉัน ไม่ ได้ ไป เที่ยว
phrûng-níi tʃán *mâi-dâai* pai thîiau
tomorrow I *no-get* go tour

3.2 If I *don't* go to school, mother won't be pleased.

ถ้า ฉัน ไม่ ได้ ไป โรงเรียน – แม่ จะ ไม่ พอ ใจ
thâa tʃán *mâi-dâai* pai roong-riian – mɛ̂ɛ tsà mâi phɔɔ-tsai
if I *no-get* go building-study – mother will no enough-heart

4 Expressing a contradiction

4.1 He *is not* Chinese, he is Thai.

เขา ไม่ ได้ เป็น คน จีน – เขา เป็น คน ไทย
kháu *mâi-dâai* pen khon-chin – kháu pen khon-thai
he *no-get* be person-China – he be person-Thai

4.2 He *doesn't* stay in Chiang Mai, he stays in Bangkok.

เขา ไม่ ได้ อยู่ ที่ เชียงใหม่ – เขา อยู่ ที่ กรุงเทพ
kháu *mâi-dâai* yùu thîi tʃiiang-mài – kháu yùu thîi krungthêep
he *no-get* stay in Chiang Mai – he stay in Bangkok

B. Highlights

> Here, we have placed **mâi-dâai** ไม่ ได้ before the action verb. When **mâi-dâai** ไม่ ได้ is placed before the action verb, it often refers to a past time action. The meaning in English is *did not* or *did not get an opportunity to*.

Depending on the context, **mâi-dâai** ไม่ ได้ can also refer to the present time or even to future time actions.

Consider the following:

1. Present time

In present time sentences **mâi-dâai** ไม่ ได้ can be translated into English as *does not* or *does not have* or *get an opportunity to*. Then, we usually need a present time word like **dĭiau-níi** เดี๋ยว นี้ *now* to make clear the action refers to the present time.

> **dĭiau-níi tʃán mâi-dâai pai roong-riian**
> เดี๋ยว นี้ ฉัน ไม่ ได้ ไป โรง เรียน
> *Nowadays, I do not go to school.*

The present time word **dĭiau-níi** เดี๋ยว นี้ *now* makes it clear that the sentence refers to the present time. The statement tells us that in the past *she has been going to school*, but nowadays *she doesn't go to school any more*.

Depending on the context, the sentence also could mean *nowadays, I do not get an opportunity to go to school*.

tɔɔn-níi tʃán mâi-dâai kin khâau tɔɔn klaang-khɯɯn lɛ́ɛu
ตอน นี้ ฉัน ไม่ ได้ กิน ข้าว ตอน กลาง คืน แล้ว
Nowadays, I don't eat at night-time any more.

If we want to express present time actions with **mâi-dâai** ไม่ ได้, then we usually need to have a present time word such as **tɔɔn-níi** ตอน นี้ in the sentence to tell us that the sentence refers to *now* or *nowadays*.

2. Past time

When **mâi-dâai** ไม่ ได้ is placed before the action verb, it often refers to a past time action. The meaning in English is *did not* or *did not get an opportunity to*.

mɯ̂ɯa-waan tʃán mâi-dâai tham arai
เมื่อวาน ฉัน ไม่ ได้ ทำ อะไร
Yesterday, I didn't do anything.

This sentence could also be translated into English as *yesterday, I did not get an opportunity to do anything*.

The time word **mɯ̂ɯa-waan** เมื่อวาน *yesterday* makes it clear that the action is referring to the past. In another context and without the time word **mɯ̂ɯa-waan** เมื่อวาน, the above sentence could mean, *I am not doing anything*.

tʃán mâi-dâai sài rɔɔng-tháu nai hɔ̂ng
ฉัน ไม่ ได้ ใส่ รอง เท้า ใน ห้อง
I didn't wear shoes in the room.

Here, the past tense is understood from the context. When **mâi-dâai** ไม่ ได้ is placed before the main verb and when there is no time word, the statement is usually understood by Thais as a past time sentence.

3. Future time

In future time sentences **mâi-dâai** ไม่ ได้ can be translated into English as *will not, not going to* or *will not get an opportunity to*. Then, we usually need a future time word like **phrûng-níi** พรุ่ง นี้ *tomorrow* to make clear the action refers to the future.

phrûng-níi tɕán mâi-dâai pai thîiau
พรุ่ง นี้ ฉัน ไม่ ได้ ไป เที่ยว
Tomorrow, I am not going out.

When talking about the future, there are a few possible translations of the above sentence in English. Contemplate on the following:

Tomorrow, I am not going to go out.

Tomorrow, I will not go out.

Tomorrow, I will not be going out.

Tomorrow, I won't have an opportunity to go out.

Tomorrow, I don't get a chance to go out.

Why so many translations? This is the nature of the English language while talking about the future. There are many ways to do it and different tenses that can be used.

In Thai, the future time word **phrûng-níi** พรุ่ง นี้ *tomorrow* in the sentence makes clear that **mâi-dâai** ไม่ ได้ refers to the future.

thâa tɕán mâi-dâai pai roong-riian, ...
ถ้า ฉัน ไม่ ได้ ไป โรงเรียน, ...
If I don't go to school ...

The "if clause" here refers to the future. This makes it clear that **mâi-dâai** ไม่ ได้ also refers to the future. Depending on the context this could be translated into English as *if I don't get an opportunity to go to school....*

4. Expressing a contradiction

mâi-dâai ไม่ ได้ can be used to express a contradiction

> **kháu mâi-dâai pen khon-chin – kháu pen khon-thai**
> เขา ไม่ ได้ เป็น คน จีน เขา เป็น คน ไทย
> *He is not Chinese, he is Thai.*

mâi-dâai ไม่ ได้ before the action verb can be used to express a contradiction, *the opposite of what was previously thought.*

This type of expression is used in situations when another person corrects someone's statement.

> **kháu mâi-dâai yùu thîi tʃiiang-mài – kháu yùu thîi krungthêep**
> เขา ไม่ ได้ อยู่ ที่ เชียงใหม่ – เขา อยู่ ที่ กรุงเทพ
> *He doesn't stay in Chiang Mai, he stays in Bangkok.*

When expressing a contradiction with **mâi-dâai** ไม่ ได้, we need to have two independent clauses. The first clause expresses a contradiction and the latter reveals the truth. See the sentences 4.1 and 4.2 above.

C. Understanding mâi-dâai ไม่ ได้

Generally, **mâi-dâai** ไม่ ได้ before the action verb can be understood as expressing a negative past tense, *did not* or *did not get an opportunity to.*

> When **mâi-dâai** ไม่ ได้ is placed directly before the action verb, its semantic boundaries are defined by the context and what other words are used with it. Depending on the context and the way the statement is said, **mâi-dâai** ไม่ ได้ can have several different meanings from the *simple negative past* to more sophisticated expressions referring to *not having future opportunities.*

When placed directly before the main verb and in the absence of time words in the sentence, Thais usually tend to understand **mâi-dâai** ไม่ ได้ as a past time phrase.

Word order:

> subject + **mâi-dâai** + verb = *did not, did not get an opportunity to*
>
> kháu + **mâi-dâai** + **pai** = *He did not go, he did not get an opportunity to go*

Basically, **mâi-dâai** ไม่ ได้, before the action verb in Thai, can have at least five different distinct meanings:

1. Without the time word, when **mâi-dâai** ไม่ ได้ is placed *before* the action verb, it often refers to the simple past, *did not*. We could also add a past time word like **mûua-waan** เมื่อวาน *yesterday* in order to specify the actual timing of the action.

2. When we add a present time word like **dǐiau-níi** เดี๋ยว นี้ *now, nowadays,* the tense changes from the past to the present, *nowadays, I don't...* See the sentences 1.1 and 1.2, page 238.

3. In many cases and depending on the context, **mâi-dâai** ไม่ ได้ before the action verb can be translated into English as *not getting the opportunity to* do something. For example, *yesterday, I did not get an opportunity to.* See the sentences 2.1 and 2.2, page 238.

4. **mâi-dâai** ไม่ ได้ can also be used in the future time phrase and the meaning is *will not*. Then, usually, we use a future time word like **phrûng-níi** พรุ่ง นี้. The meaning is then *tomorrow, I am not* or *tomorrow, I won't get an opportunity to...* When the sentence starts with the if clause **thâa** ถ้า *if*, then the sentence also refers to the future. The meaning is *if I won't..., then...* See the sentences 3.1 and 3.2, page 239.

5. In addition, **mâi-dâai** ไม่ ได้ can be placed before the action verb to express *a contradiction*, the opposite of what was earlier thought.

When expressing a contradiction with **mâi-dâai** ไม่ ได้, we need two independent clauses. The first clause expresses the contradiction and latter reveals the truth, *the opposite of what was previously thought*. See the sentences 4.1 and 4.2, page 239.

D. Conclusion

> Key: Place **mâi-dâai** ไม่ ได้ before the action verb to express meanings like *I did not* or *I did not get an opportunity to*.

1. The usage of **mâi-dâai** ไม่ ได้ before the action verb is grammatically slightly complicated since it can express past time, present time, future time and also a contradiction.

2. As far as **mâi-dâai** ไม่ ได้ phrase before the action verb is concerned, it is used in a similar way as **dâai** ได้. However, the usage of the **mâi-dâai** ไม่ ได้ phrase is somewhat more sophisticated. It takes some time and effort to comprehend it totally and understand how Thai people use it in everyday situations.

3. **mâi-dâai** ไม่ ได้ before the action verb is perhaps best learned by using it in the sentence. In the next Language hints section, we give you many more examples and hope you will get the feeling for it.

4. It may help if you try to think as Thai people do. For them, **mâi-dâai** ไม่ ได้ before the action verb simply means *"did not get to"*.

   It can also be translated into English as *did not, did not have* or *get an opportunity to*. In the absence of time words, **mâi-dâai** ไม่ ได้ before the action verb is often understood as a past tense by Thais.

5. In order to get the tense more clear and exact, time words like **mûua-waan** เมื่อ วาน *yesterday*, **dǐiau-níi** เดี๋ยว นี้ *now* or **phrûng-níi** พรุ่ง นี้ *tomorrow* are commonly used.

E. Language hints

> Here, we illustrate that the meaning of **mâi-dâai** ไม่ ได้ is very much understood from the context and whether it is placed *before* or *after* the main verb. Note also that other words used together with **mâi-dâai** ไม่ ได้ can change the meaning and the tense in Thai. This is quite important to understand.

In the following sentences, there will be a lot of information that can be a bit challenging to comprehend in detail. Many a time, there is only a subtle difference when we use **mâi-dâai** ไม่ ได้ in different contexts.

The correct usage of **mâi-dâai** ไม่ ได้ helps you to better interact with Thai people. This underlines the importance of learning to speak Thai intuitively as native Thai people do.

Consider the following:

> **1** I *didn't* go anywhere. I am staying here!
> ฉัน ไม่ ได้ ไป ไหน – ฉัน อยู่ ที่ นี่
> tʃǎn *mâi-dâai* pai nǎi – tʃǎn yùu thîi-nîi
> I *no-get* go somewhere – I stay place-this

This sentence expresses a contradiction with **mâi-dâai** ไม่ ได้.

mâi-dâai ไม่ ได้ is put before the action verb. It is used to contradict the earlier statement. The second sentence reveals the truth.

> **2** Nowadays, I *don't get the opportunity to* go anywhere.
> เดี๋ยว นี้ ฉัน ไม่ ได้ ไป ไหน
> dǐiau-níi tʃǎn *mâi-dâai* pai nǎi
> moment-this I *no-get* go somewhere

This sentence expresses *getting an opportunity* with **mâi-dâai** ไม่ ได้.

Here, **mâi-dâai** ไม่ ได้ is used with the present time word. **dǐiau-níi** เดี๋ยว นี้ *now* at the beginning of the sentence is used to emphasize the present time.

Depending on the context, this sentence could also be translated into English as *now, I am not going anywhere.*

> **3** I *didn't get an opportunity to* go there often.
> ฉัน ไม่ ได้ ไป ที่ นั่น บ่อยๆ
> tʃǎn *mâi-dâai* pai thîi-nân bɔ̀ɔi-bɔ̀ɔi
> I *no-get* go place-that often-often

This sentence expresses a past tense with **mâi-dâai** ไม่ ได้.

We have placed a time word of frequency **bɔ̀ɔi-bɔ̀ɔi** บ่อยๆ *often* at the end of the sentence.

Depending on the context, this statement could also be translated into English as *I don't go there often* or *I didn't go there often.*

> **4** Tomorrow, I *am not going* anywhere.
> พรุ่ง นี้ ฉัน ไม่ ได้ ไป ไหน
> phrûng-níi tʃán *mâi-dâai* pai nǎi
> tomorrow I *no-get* go somewhere

This sentence expresses a future tense with **mâi-dâai** ไม่ ได้.

Here, **mâi-dâai** ไม่ ได้ is used with the future time word. **phrûng-níi** พรุ่ง นี้ *tomorrow* at the beginning of the sentences is used to emphasize the future.

This sentence can also be translated into English as *tomorrow, I won't have an opportunity to go anywhere.*

> **5** Tomorrow, I *cannot* go anywhere.
> พรุ่ง นี้ ฉัน ไป ไหน ไม่ ได้
> phrûng-níi tʃán pai nǎi *mâi-dâai*
> tomorrow I go somewhere *no-can*

This sentence expresses *not being able to* with **mâi-dâai** ไม่ ได้.

This sentence can also be translated into English as *tomorrow, I am not allowed to go anywhere.*

When **mâi-dâai** ไม่ ได้ is placed after the action verb, the meaning is that the action is not possible *whatever the reason*.

> **6** *Not everybody* is going.
> ไม่ ได้ ไป ทุก คน
> *mâi-dâai* pai thúk-khon
> *no-get* go every-person

This sentence refers to the future. Somebody will be going, not everybody.

The context and how the statement is said reveals the tense. **mâi-dâai** ไม่ได้ can be used before the action verb to express the future time.

This statement could also be translated into English as *not everybody has an opportunity to go, not everybody had an opportunity to go* or *not everybody went*.

Nobody went.

ทุก คน ไม่ ได้ ไป
thúk-khon *mâi-dâai* pai
every-person *no-get* go

When we place **thúk-khon** ทุก คน *everybody* at the beginning of the sentence, the meaning changes.

Now, the statement is translated into English as *nobody went*. It is a past time statement.

This sentence can also be translated into English as *nobody had an opportunity to go*.

Nobody can go.

ทุก คน ไป ไม่ ได้
thúk-khon pai *mâi-dâai*
every-person *no-can* go

This sentence can also be translated into English as *nobody is permitted to go* or *nobody is able to go*.

Generally, **mâi-dâai** ไม่ได้ after the action verb can be understood as the action is not possible *whatever the reason*.

Secret 14

 B) Just for fun, there are at least 10 ways to express the negative statement *"not drinking alcohol"*. Every statement has a slightly different meaning.

Consider the following:

I *have not been* drinking.
ผม ไม่ ได้ กิน เหล้า
phŏm *mâi-dâai* kin lâu
I *no-get* eat alcohol

This statement says that *he has not been drinking*. This statement expresses *a recent past time activity* that didn't happen.

Often in casual speech, Thais use the word **kin** กิน *to eat* for drinking also.

Depending on the context, this sentence can also be understood as *I didn't get an opportunity to drink*.

Nowadays, I *don't drink* alcohol any more.
เดี๋ยว นี้ ผม ไม่ ได้ ดื่ม เหล้า แล้ว
dǐau-níi phŏm *mâi-dâai* dùum lâu léɛu
moment-this I *no-get* drink alcohol already

This statement tells us that he had been *drinking before*, but nowadays he *doesn't drink any more*. The statement tells us that *he has stopped drinking*.

The word **dùum** ดื่ม *to drink* is used for drinking but not for eating.

Depending on the context, this sentence can also be understood as *nowadays, I "don't get to" drink alcohol any more*.

> **3**
> I *can't* drink alcohol.
> ผม ดื่ม เหล้า ไม่ ได้
> phŏm dùum lâu *mâi-dâai*
> I drink alcohol *no-can*

He can't drink alcohol *whatever the reason.* Maybe he *doesn't have permission* to drink, or he thinks *it tastes terrible,* or he has *some health reason* for not drinking.

> **4**
> I *don't* drink alcohol.
> ผม กิน เหล้า ไม่ เป็น
> phŏm kin lâu *mâi-pen*
> I eat alcohol *no-skill*

When **pen** เป็น is used in connection with foods and drinks, the translation into English is slightly different. **pen** เป็น means *having skill to do something.*

The literal translation into English is *I do not know how to drink alcohol* or *I do not have the skill to drink alcohol.*

However, the more correct translation into English would be *I don't drink alcohol, I am not accustomed to drink,* or *it is not my habit to drink alcohol.*

> **5**
> I *don't* drink alcohol.
> ผม ไม่ ดื่ม เหล้า
> phŏm *mâi* dùum lâu
> I *no* drink alcohol

This is a blunt statement saying that *he doesn't drink alcohol*. Compare this sentence with sentence 4. There is a clear difference in meaning in Thai. However, the translation into English could be the same or very similar.

> **6**
>
> I *don't have the strength to* drink alcohol.
>
> ผม ดื่ม เหล้า ไม่ ไหว
> phŏm dùum lâu *mâi-wăi*
> I drink alcohol *no-strength*

He can't drink alcohol because *he is too weak* to do so. Maybe, he is sick or just tired of drinking.

> **7**
>
> I *do not want* to drink alcohol.
>
> ผม ไม่ อยาก กิน เหล้า
> phŏm *mâi yàak* kin lâu
> I *no want* eat alcohol

This statement says that *he doesn't want* or *doesn't like to drink alcohol*. There is maybe a good reason for his standpoint.

> **8**
>
> I *have never* drunk alcohol.
>
> ผม ไม่ เคย ดื่ม เหล้า
> phŏm *mâi khəəi* dùum lâu
> I *no once* drink alcohol

This statement says that *he has never tasted* or *drank alcohol*.

> **9** *Do not* drink alcohol!
> อย่า ได้ ดื่ม เหล้า
> *yàa-dâai* dùum lâu
> *no-get* drink alcohol

This is a command, *do not drink alcohol!* The order is coming from someone else.

dâai ได้ here, after the word **yàa** อย่า *do not,* makes the statement to be a clear and strong command.

> **10** *Please, do not* drink alcohol!
> อย่า ดื่ม เหล้า ได้ ไหม
> yàa dùum lâu *dâai-mái*
> no drink alcohol *can-question*

The command can be made softer by putting **dâai-mái** ได้ ไหม at the end of the sentence.

F. Simple advice

> When **mâi-dâai** ไม่ ได้ is used in the sentence, we need to pay close attention in order to get the right meaning. **mâi-dâai** ไม่ ได้ can have several different meanings depending on the context and other words it is used with.

When **mâi-dâai** ไม่ ได้ is placed after the action verb, it expresses meanings such as *cannot, not being able to* or *not having permission to*. In fact, the action is not possible *whatever the reason*. See also Secret 13.

When **mâi-dâai** ไม่ ได้ is placed before the action verb, it often expresses past time activities and can be translated into English as *did not* or *did not have an opportunity to* do something. Thais would usually think in terms of "not getting" the action in question. If **dâai** ได้ is dropped, the meaning is different.

If we use the single word **mâi** ไม่ *no* to negate the statement, then it is usually a direct blunt statement with some future connection.

Examples:

> **1**   mâi ไม่ + action verb
>
> I *am not* going anywhere.
>
> ฉัน ไม่ ไป ไหน
> tʃán *mâi* pai nǎi
> I *no* go somewhere

Here, **dâai** ได้ is dropped and **mâi** ไม่ *no* is put before the action verb to negate the statement. **mâi** ไม่ *no* before the action verb often has some future connotation. The decision about the possible future action has been made.

Depending on the context, this sentence could also be translated into English as *I won't go anywhere* or *I am not going to go anywhere*.

> **2**   mâi-dâai ไม่ ได้ + action verb
>
> I *didn't* go anywhere.
>
> ฉัน ไม่ ได้ ไป ไหน
> tʃán *mâi-dâai* pai nǎi
> I *no-get* go somewhere

mâi-dâai ไม่ ได้ before the action verb often refers to the past.

Here, **mâi-dâai** ไม่ ได้ is placed before the action verb to express meanings like *I didn't* or *I didn't have an opportunity to go anywhere*.

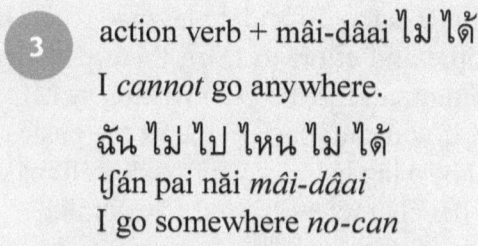

action verb + mâi-dâai ไม่ ได้

I *cannot* go anywhere.

ฉัน ไม่ ไป ไหน ไม่ ได้
tʃán pai nǎi *mâi-dâai*
I go somewhere *no-can*

Here, **mâi-dâai** ไม่ ได้ expresses a different meaning. When **mâi-dâai** ไม่ ได้ is placed after the action verb, it expresses meanings such as *cannot, not being able to* or *not having permission to*.

In this book, we have already touched the subject of Thai tenses. In the next Book II *Learning Thai Tenses with **dâai*** ได้ (Secrets 15–22), we shall study in detail how to make sentences which refer to the past, present or future time.

A. Introduction to sounds and Thai transliteration

Many western students think that it is too difficult to learn to read Thai letters and do not invest the time and effort to learn them. It is true that you do not need to have a command of the Thai writing system in order to speak Thai. However, if you can master at least the basics of the Thai writing system, it will be a big help for your studies. It makes sense, therefore, to learn the Thai characters from the beginning.

Western letters can only be used as an aid in learning to speak Thai. You should not use western letters in writing Thai sentences. There are so many different ways to transliterate that your effort would be fruitless. Thais would be unlikely to understand what you had written. In Thailand, western letters are only used in names and road signs.

Western letters may aid your understanding of how certain Thai words are pronounced, but if you do take the trouble to learn to read and write the Thai script, Thai people will be very impressed!

Note that we do not review the tones in this section. We give, however, the correct tone symbols in transliterations. We transliterate Thai sounds with western letters or international phonetic symbols. This process is called phonetic writing, transliteration and sometimes also romanization.

This presentation includes all consonant and vowel sounds used in central Thai. However, there are many more Thai consonants, and also some vowel sounds can be written in several different ways.

In Thai there are altogether 20 consonant sounds and 18 pure vowel sounds.

By knowing how new sounds are made both in theory and practice, you will become more confident in learning Thai. Then practise and adjust your speaking until you can make new sounds correctly.

Introduction to sounds and Thai transliteration 257

If in doubt, please review this section and also read the book *22 Secrets of Learning Thai – Complete Guide to Sounds, Tones and Thai Writing System*.

1 Thai consonant sounds

Many foreign words borrowed from Pali, Sanskrit or Khmer use rare consonants for common sounds. Hence, in the Thai alphabet list, 42 consonants make only 20 different consonant sounds.

Basically, there are three types of consonant sounds in Thai, namely stop consonant sounds, fricative consonant sounds and sonorant consonant sounds. This distinction is very important in Thai in order to understand the Thai writing system and tones.

1.1 Stop consonant sounds

Stop consonant sounds can be divided into four basic categories, namely aspirated consonants, unaspirated consonants, affricate consonants and voiced consonants.

1.1.1 Aspirated stop consonants

Aspiration means that there is a puff of air coming out of your mouth when you produce the sound. Stop consonants are produced in such a way that air is first stopped by the lips or by the tongue and then released by a plosive.

phɔɔ พ, thɔɔ ท, khɔɔ ค

- the letter **h** is used to denote the fact that the sound is aspirated with the puff of air

Thai words:
phaan	พาน	*tray*
phûng	ผึ้ง	*bee*
phɛɛng	แพง	*expensive*
tháhǎan	ทหาร	*soldier*

thŭng	ถุง	*bag*
thêep	เทพ	*God*
khwaai	ควาย	*water buffalo*
khài	ไข่	*egg*
khon	คน	*person*

Similar English sounds: **P**eter, **p**erson, **p**aper, **t**ime, **t**ake, **t**one, **k**iss, **k**ey, **k**eep

Rating: Good

- these sounds are not difficult for English speakers since similar consonant sounds in English are always aspirated at the beginning of a word or a syllable
- put your hand in front of the mouth, and feel that there is a puff of air coming when you say these words either in Thai or in English

1.1.2 Unaspirated stop consonants

When the sound is unaspirated, it means that there isn't any puff of air coming out of your mouth when you produce this sound. The sound is first stopped by the lips or by the tongue and then released in such a way, that there is no any puff of air coming out of your mouth when you make this consonant sound. The air is somehow stopped in the glottis. This is called in phonetic terms a glottal stop.

pɔɔ ป, tɔɔ ต, kɔɔ ก

Thai words:

plaa	ปลา	*fish*
pìt	ปิด	*to close*
pìip	ปีบ	*cork tree*
tàu	เต่า	*turtle*
tên	เต้น	*to dance*
tiin	ตีน	*foot* (not polite)
kài	ไก่	*chicken*

Introduction to sounds and Thai transliteration

kɛ̀	แกะ	*to unwrap*
kɛ̀ɛ	แก่	*to be old*

Similar English sounds: s**p**eak, s**p**ell, s**p**y, s**t**op, s**t**ink, s**t**ate, s**k**in, s**k**ate, s**k**y

Rating: Not very good

- the tricky point is that in English we don't have unaspirated consonant sounds at the beginning of a word or a syllable
- we have therefore taken as examples similar consonant sounds in the middle of the word where the English aspiration is weak
- put your hand in front of the mouth, and make sure that there is no puff of air coming when you say these Thai words
- you may need some practice before getting the pronunciation of these words right without any puff of air. Do no hesitate to consult your Thai teacher

1.1.3 Affricate stop consonants

Affricate consonant sounds consist of two sounds at the beginning of the word, **tʃ** or **ts**. They can be either aspirated or unaspirated.

These affricate stop consonant sounds are produced in such a way that the air is first stopped by the tongue and then released.

tʃɔɔ ช and **tsɔɔ** จ

In Thai there are two affricate stop consonant sounds, **tʃ** as in the word **tʃ**ɔɔp ชอบ and **ts** as in the word **ts**ing จริง. The first sound in Thai is aspirated, and the second is unaspirated. English also has two affricate sounds, **tʃ** as in the word **ch**ild and **dʒ** as in the **j**ob. The first sound in English is aspirated, and the second is voiced.

English stop sounds at the beginning of a word are usually divided into aspirated and voiced. In Thai, the similar initial sounds are aspirated or unaspirated.

tʃɔɔ ช

Thai words:

tʃáang	ช้าง	elephant
tʃǐng	ฉิ่ง	cymbals
tʃɛ́ɛ	แฉ	to reveal, to show

Similar English sounds: **ch**ild, **ch**oose, **ch**apter

Rating: Good

- with this sound English speakers usually don't have any problem
- you may use the English sound and there should not be any problem
- put your hand in front of the mouth, and feel that there is a puff of air coming when you say these words either in Thai or in English

tsɔɔ จ

The sound **tsɔɔ จ** is perhaps the most misunderstood Thai sound among non-native speakers. Therefore, we try to explain it here in detail.

This Thai sound **tsɔɔ จ** is transliterated in many ways, examples include: **j**, **ch**, **c**, **dsch**. The most correct way to transliterate this sound would be to use the international phonetic symbol **tɕ**. It is not known very well however and therefore seldom used. We have decided to use simply **ts**.

Thai words:

tsaan	จาน	plate
tsùm	จุ่ม	to dip
tsùu	จู่	to rush

Similar English sounds for **tsɔɔ จ**: **g**in, **j**oy, **ts**unami

Introduction to sounds and Thai transliteration

Rating: Not very good

- the letter **j**, as in the English word **joy**, is often given as an example. This is, however, not quite right, since the English consonant **j** is voiced, but the Thai sound **ts** จ is unvoiced
- note that if you pronounce the word **ts**unami as it is written and not like **s**unami, you are close
- make sure that you start with **t**-sound and then glide into **s**-sound. Put your hand in front of the mouth, and feel that there is not much air coming from your mouth when you say the above Thai words
- note also that English sounds, which are not aspirated at the beginning of the word are usually voiced. This Thai sound **tsɔɔ** จ is not voiced, not aspirated but unaspirated
- **ts**unami is a foreign word and is pronounced in several different ways by English speakers and therefore it is not a very good example
- the same type of foreign sound is the Russian word **ts**ar
- why is this sound difficult for English speakers? The reason is because there is no such a sound at the beginning of English words. The same sound exists frequently at the end of the word in English. Good examples are: **Let's**, **cats**, **hats**, **bits** etc...
- note, however, if you pronounce this sound as in the English word **job**, you will be understood by Thais since there is no similar voiced sound in Thai for it to be confused with. In that case your pronunciation is not quite correct

1.1.4 Voiced stop consonants

Voiced sounds in Thai and in English are not aspirated. They are produced in such a way that vocal folds are vibrating. The sound is first stopped by the lips or by the tongue and then released.

bɔɔ บ, dɔɔ ด

Thai words:

bai máai	ใบ ไม้	leaf
bin	บิน	to fly
bìip	บีบ	to squeeze
dèk	เด็ก	child
dù	ดุ	to scold
duu	ดู	to look, to see
din	ดิน	land, earth

Similar English sounds: **b**aby, **b**anana, **b**ig, **d**inner, **d**uck, **d**ance

Rating: Good

- here there is no problem at all. The English sounds are very similar to the Thai sounds
- note, however, that at the beginning of a word or a syllable the consonant sounds in English are either voiced or aspirated, but in Thai they can be aspirated, unaspirated and also voiced

1.2 Fricative consonant sounds

Fricative consonant sounds are produced in such a way that the air is not stopped but directed through a narrow channel. The turbulent airflow makes a friction. In Thai there are only two fricative sounds, namely **f** and **s**. Fricative consonants sounds in Thai are unvoiced.

In English there are three fricative sounds, **f**, **s** and **z**. In Thai the voiced counterpart **z** does not exist.

In order to be complete, we need to add one more fricative sound, the glottal fricative sound **h**, which is used similarly in Thai and in English.

Introduction to sounds and Thai transliteration

fɔɔ ฟ, ซ sɔɔ, hɔɔ ฮ

Thai words:

fan	ฟัน	*teeth*
făa	ฝา	*lid, cover*
fŭung	ฝูง	*group, flock*
sôo	โซ่	*chain*
sŭua	เสือ	*tiger*
sŭun	ศูนย์	*zero*
nók hûuk	นกฮูก	*owl*
hìip	หีบ	*chest*
hε̂ɛng	แห้ง	*dry*

Similar English sounds: **f**ive, **f**ax, **f**orm, **s**even, **s**imple, **s**ame, **h**e, **h**ave, **h**ost

Rating: Good

- if you use the English pronunciation for these three sounds, there should be no problems

1.3 Sonorant consonant sounds

The term sonorant sound means that the sound can be prolonged without any difficulty. The sound is not stopped by lips or by tongue. Sonorant sounds play a very important role as far as the Thai writing system is concerned. They are:

mɔɔ ม, nɔɔ น, lɔɔ ล, rɔɔ ร, ngɔɔ ง, yɔɔ ย and wɔɔ ว

Most sonorant sounds are pronounced in a similar way in Thai and in English.

If you use the English pronunciation for the following sonorant consonant sounds, there should be no problems.

There are, however, two sounds that we would like to explain in more detail, namely **rɔɔ** ร and **ngɔɔ** ง.

mɔɔ ม

Thai words:

máa	ม้า	*horse*
mǎu	เหมา	*to presume, to rent*
mâai	ม่าย	*widow*

Similar English sounds: **m**other, **m**ake, **m**ain

Rating: Good

nɔɔ น

nǔu	หนู	*mouse*
nâu	เน่า	*rotten*
nǎau	หนาว	*cold*

Similar English sounds: **n**ine, **n**ice, **n**ot

Rating: Good

lɔɔ ล

ling	ลิง	*monkey*
lǎi	ไหล	*flow*
lǎai	หลาย	*many*

Similar English sounds: **l**ine, **l**ips, **l**oose

Rating: Good

rɔɔ ร

Thai words:

rɯɯa	เรือ	*boat*
rai	ไร	*something*
raai	ราย	*item*

Similar English sounds: **r**ed, **r**ead, **r**ipe

Rating: Not very good

- many Thai speakers substitute this **r** ร-sound with the **l** ล-sound as in the English world like. So, it is quite common that Thai is spoken without the correct Thai **r** ร-sound
- when the correct **r** ร-sound is used by Thais, it is not exactly the same sound as the English **r**-sound
- Thai **r** is rolled more like the Spanish **r**
- some English speakers may produce this sound differently depending on origin of the country, education etc...

ngɔɔ ง

Thai words:

nguu	งู	*snake*
ngong	งง	*to be confused*
ngóong	โง้ง	*to be bent*

English words: ki**ng**, si**ng**i**ng**, fi**ng**er

Rating: Not very good

- this sound **ng** ง appears in several combinations in the English language
- however, it can prove quite difficult for English speaking learners to use this sound at the beginning of a word. This shows how strongly language skills are based on habits
- you may practise this sound by saying the first part of the word si**nging** silently and the second part loudly

yɔɔ ย

Thai words:

yák	ยักษ์	*giant*
yím	ยิ้ม	*smile*
yîiam	เยี่ยม	*excellent*

Similar English sounds: **y**ellow, **y**es, **y**ear

Rating: Good

wɔɔ ว

Thai words:
wĕɛn	แหวน	*ring*
wai	ไว	*fast*
wăai	หวาย	*wicker palm*

Similar English sounds: **w**omen, **w**ife, **w**inter

Rating: Good

2 Thai vowel sounds

In Thai there are 9 short and 9 long pure vowel sounds. With these 18 vowel sounds you will be able to make all Thai vowel sounds including diphthongs and all other vowel combinations.

The main obstacle with the Thai vowel sounds for English speakers is to learn to separate short vowel sounds from their long counterparts. In Thai vowels are produced clearly short or long.

In English the pronunciation of vowels can vary depending on the person and the accent. Often in English the short vowels can be prolonged or long vowels shortened without loosing the meaning of the word. This can't be done with Thai vowels.

Note also that when we transliterate the vowel sounds, we write a short sound with one symbol and a long sound with two symbols. Some transliteration systems do not separate short and long vowels. Then there is no way to know how to pronounce those vowels. If you don't pronounce Thai vowels clearly, Thai people will have difficulty to understand you.

Introduction to sounds and Thai transliteration

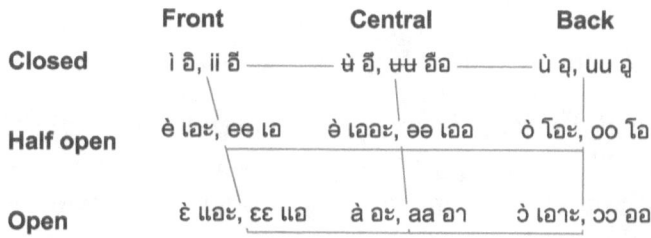

ì อิ and ii อี

Learn to separate the short ì อิ-sound from its long counterpart ii อี.

Thai words:

bì	บิ	to break off
bìip	บีบ	to squeeze, to press
pìt	ปิด	to close
pìip	ปีบ	cork tree
bin	บิน	to fly
biin	บีน	(only a sound, no meaning)

Similar English sounds for short ì อิ: h**i**ppy, th**i**nk, s**i**t

Similar English sounds for long ii อี: s**ee**, m**ea**t, t**ea**ch

Rating: Good

- if you use the English pronunciation for the short ì อิ and long ii อี -sounds, there should be no problems
- just make sure that the short sound is short and the long sound clearly long
- note also that some English speakers, particularly Americans, tend to make this sound towards **e**-sound as in the English word p**e**t

ึ อึ and ืือ

Learn to separate the short ึ อึ-sound from its long counterpart ืือ อืือ.

It is often said that there is no comparable sound in English for these two sounds. This is not quite true, since some English speakers, even in England and USA, seem to use a similar sound with words like c**ou**ld, sh**ou**ld, g**oo**d, c**u**te, f**ew** and r**u**de. Others pronounce the same sound differently.

Thai words:

phừng	ผึ่ง	*to dry, to expose*
phừưn	ผืน	*prickly*
bûng	บึ้ง	*to be serious*
pûưn	ปืน	*eruption on the skin*
phûng	ผึ้ง	*bee*
phǔưn	ผืน	*sheet*

Similar English sounds for short ึ อึ: sh**ou**ld, g**oo**d, w**ou**ld

Similar English sounds for long ืือ อืือ: c**u**te, f**ew**, r**u**de

Rating: Not good

- listen to the audio and try to adjust your sound to conform with the Thai sound
- if you are facing difficulties, we would advise you to find a good native Thai teacher to get this sound right since you can't directly use the English sounds
- remember to make a short sound short and a long vowel sound clearly long

ù อุ and uu อู

Note that the long English **uu** อู-sound is sometimes pronounced differently by different English speakers. Some may use a version similar

Introduction to sounds and Thai transliteration

to the Thai sound, **ʉʉ** อือ. This happens often with words like new, dew, good, two.

Do not mix up these two sounds **ù** อุ and **ʉ** อึ or **uu** อู and **ʉʉ** อือ. In Thai, they are clearly different sounds. In English, the distinction is not so clear.

Thai words:

fùn	ฝุ่น	*dust*
fŭung	ฝูง	*group*
pù	ปุ	*to repair*
pùu	ปู่	*grandfather*
bun	บุญ	*merit*
phuun	พูน	*to pile up*

Similar English sounds for short **ù** อุ: l**oo**k, p**u**t, f**oo**t

Similar English sounds for long **uu** อู: c**oo**l, s**oo**n, d**o**

Rating: Quite good, but pay attention

- do not mix up the short **ù** อุ with the short **ʉ** อึ
- do not mix up the long **uu** อู with the long **ʉʉ** อือ
- they are made in a similar way. **ù** อุ and **uu** อู are made with rounded lips and **ʉ** อึ and **ʉʉ** อือ are made with unrounded lips

è เอะ and **ee** เอ

The short **è** เอะ and the long **ee** เอ-sounds do not exist in their pure form in Standard English.

Thai words:

thét	เท็จ	*false, incorrect*
thêet	เทศ	*foreign*
pen	เป็น	*to be*

pheen	เพล	lunch time (monk)
pèt	เป็ด	duck
thêep	เทพ	god, divine being

Similar English sounds for short è เอะ: pet, said, bread

Rating: Quite good, but pay attention

Similar English words for long ee เอ: pale, paint, sail

Rating: Not very good

- some English speakers pronounce the short è เอะ sound in English close to the Thai sound ɛ̀ แอะ while others may pronounce it differently
- note that in Thai vowel sounds can't be changed in any way. They need to be pronounced clearly
- the long ee เอ sound doesn't exist in its pure form in Standard English
- if you pronounce the ee เอ sound as in the English word pale like peeil without the i-sound, you are close to this Thai sound
- listen to the audio and ask your native Thai teacher to correct your pronunciation in order to learn to get these two sounds exactly right

ə̀ เออะ and əə เออ

Learn to separate this short ə̀ เออะ-sound from its long counterpart əə เออ.

These two sounds appear in English often with the consonant r. In order to get the Thai sound right you should not pronounce the r-sound.

Thai words:
də̂n	เดิ้น	smart (slang)
dəən	เดิน	to walk

Introduction to sounds and Thai transliteration

tə̀	เตอะ	(only a sound, no meaning)
təəm	เติม	*to fill, to add*
bə̀ng	เบิ่ง	*to look* (Isaan dialect)
pə̀ət	เปิด	*to open*

Similar English sounds for short **ə̀** เออะ: ab**ou**t, teach**er**, **A**nglia

Similar English sounds for long **əə** เออ: h**er**, b**ir**d, b**ur**n

Rating: Quite good, but pay attention

- if you speak American English, please be aware that you should pronounce short **ə̀** เออะ and long **əə** เออ-sounds without the **r**-sound. If in doubt, ask your native teacher to help you get these sounds exactly right

ò โอะ and oo โอ

Be aware that in Thai, long and short vowels are pronounced the same, only the duration is different. These two sounds in English are usually turned into a vowel combination such as **ou** or **əu**.

Please make sure that you are able to understand and produce these sounds correctly. You need to learn to make these sounds, short and long, without the **u**-sound.

Thai words:

son	ซน	*to be naughty*
soon	โซน	*zone, area*
sòt	สด	*fresh*
sòot	โสด	*single, unmarried*
tòt	ตด	*to fart*
dòot	โดด	*to jump*

Similar English sounds for short **ò** โอะ: f**o**lk, r**o**ll, b**o**lt

Similar English sounds for long **oo** โอ: g**o**, hell**o**, l**aw**

Rating: Not very good

- the short **ò** โอะ and the long **oo** โอ sounds do not exist in their pure form in Standard English
- for the short **ò** โอะ sound you need to learn to say the English word f**o**lk, without the **ù** อุ-sound
- for the long **oo** โอ you must learn to say the English word *go* without the **ù** อุ-sound as g**oo**
- make this long **oo** โอ-sound longer than the short **ò** โอะ. It is close to the long ɔɔ ออ-sound as in the English word **law**

ὲ แอะ and εε แอ

Learn to separate the short **ὲ** แอะ-sound from its long counterpart **εε** แอ.

Thai words:

tʃὲ	แฉะ	wet
tʃɛɛ	แฉ	to reveal, to show
tsὲ	แจะ	sound of chewing
tsɛɛk	แจก	to hand out
kὲ	แกะ	to unwrap
kɛɛ	แก่	to be old

Similar English sounds for short **ὲ** แอะ: c**a**t, h**a**ng, **a**t

Similar English sounds for long **εε** แอ: s**a**d, b**a**d, m**a**d

Rating: Quite good, but pay attention

- if you use the English sound as in the word c**a**t for the short **ὲ** แอะ- sound, you are quite close

Introduction to sounds and Thai transliteration

- if you use the English sound as in the word b**a**d for the long ɛɛ แอ, you are quite close
- Note, however, that some English speakers tend to pronounce the long ɛɛ แอ as in the English word b**a**d shorter than it is pronounced in Thai. Make sure that you always pronounce long vowel sounds long in Thai.

à อะ and aa อา

Note that in Thai, it is very important to maintain the correct length of a vowel. When the vowel length changes, the meaning of the word changes as well. In English the length of the vowel can be changed without loosing the meaning.

Thai words:

khá	ค่ะ	ending particle
khâa	ค่า	*price*
kàt	กัด	*to bite*
kàat	กาด	*market* (Northern dialect)
khát	คัด	*to select, to copy*
khàat	ขาด	*to be missing*

Similar English sounds for short **à** อะ: b**u**t, r**u**n, fl**oo**d

Rating: Good

Similar English sounds for long **aa** อา: f**a**ther, v**a**st, p**a**ssport

Rating: Quite good, but pay attention

- for the short Thai **à** อะ sound the English sound may be used without any difficulty as in the word r**u**n
- however, some English speakers, particularly Americans, tend to pronounce the long **aa** อา-sound similar to the sound in the English word s**a**d, written phonetically as sɛɛd. They tend to say pɛɛsport instead of paasport. You need to be careful not to

change the quality of the sound when you produce these short and long vowels in Thai
- listen to the audio and then check with your native Thai teacher so that you can pronounce these two sounds clearly and exactly right

เ̀าะ เอาะ and ออ ออ

Learn to distinguish the short เ̀าะ เอาะ-sound from its long counterpart ออ ออ. Note that in Thai the difference between long and short vowel is only the length of the sound.

In English, however, changing the length of the vowel sound makes often qualitatively different sound as it is the case with these two sounds.

You also need to learn to distinguish เ̀าะ เอาะ and ออ ออ from โ̀ะ โอะ and โอ โอ. Even though these sounds are quite close, you need to learn to hear, understand and reproduce the difference.

Thai words:

hông hông	ห้อง	room
hɔ̌ɔm	หอม	to smell
hông-gong	ฮ่องกง	Hong Kong
hɔ̀ɔ	ห่อ	package
tông	ต้อง	must
thɔ́ɔng	ท้อง	stomach

Similar English sounds for short เ̀าะ เอาะ: n**o**t, g**o**t, s**o**ft

Rating: Not very good

Similar English sounds for long ออ ออ: **a**ll, c**au**ght, l**aw**

Rating: Quite good

- standard English does not have the short เ̀าะ เอาะ-sound in its pure form

- one way to explain the short ɔ̀ เอาะ-sound is to use the long ɔɔ ออ-sound as in the word l**aw** but make it short. You may need help from a native teacher to get this sound right
- if you make the long ɔɔ ออ-sound as in the English word l**aw**, you will be quite close. In Thai, this vowel is perhaps pronounced more open than the similar vowel sound in English. More open means that you open your mouth a bit more
- do not mix up these two sounds, short ɔ̀ เอาะ and short ò โอะ
- do not mix up these two sounds, long ɔɔ ออ and long oo โอ
- they are made in the similar way

B. Summary of some useful grammar terms

I Grammar

In every language, we need being able to make sounds in such a way that other people understand what we are saying. We also need being able to put words together in such a way that sentences make sense and sound right. As an adult learner, this requires some conscious and active effort on your part.

When you are learning a second language as a child, you are growing into it. Learning a second language as an adult is a different process. The learning process is not that intuitive any more. Your brain also wants to understand what you are learning. If the correct way is not readily available to you, your brain will understand things in its own way. In other words, it makes assumptions, right or wrong, from point of view of your own native language. Since Thai uses a different kind of syntax to English, the assumptions made may not be valid. You need to think the way Thai people do in order to speak Thai fluently.

1.1 Phonetics

Phonetics is concerned with the sounds of the language. This is quite important since English sounds cannot be directly transferred into Thai. This is true particularly with the vowel sounds. If you want to be understood by Thais, you need being able to produce correct Thai sounds.

You can also find more comprehensive explanation of Thai sounds in the book *22 Secrets of Learning Thai – Complete Guide to Sounds, Tones and Thai Writing System*.

1.2 Transliteration

Transliteration is a way to write Thai sounds with western letters and international phonetic symbols. This helps you to get sounds right since it may take a long time for you to able to read the Thai script properly. See more about the transliteration of Thai sounds at the end of this book.

1.3 Syntax

Syntax is concerned with the structure of the language, how the words are put together in the sentence. This is important since the Thai language uses a different type of syntax from English.

1.4 Semantics

Semantics is concerned with the meaning of words and sentences. This is important since one word can have several different semantic meanings. **dâai** ได้ is a very good example of this type of word. It may change the semantic meaning when placed in different positions in a sentence.

1.5 Semantic boundary

We use the term *semantic boundary* to describe the fact that we need to use different English words in order to define the meaning of the verb **dâai** ได้. We need to use English words such as *to get, to receive,* *can, being permitted to, to have an opportunity to* etc. to grasp the correct meaning of **dâai** ได้ when placed in different positions in a sentence.

2 Parts of speech

When describing the structure of the Thai language, we need to know a few basic terms, usually called in English *parts of speech*.

2.1 Nouns

2.1.1 Common nouns

The word *common noun* is a word used for things such as *dogs, cats, cars, computers*. They have a physical form and they can be touched. **dâai** ได้ can be placed before a noun in order to have a distinct meaning, *to get*. See Secret 1.

2.1.2 Abstract nouns

An *abstract noun* is a word used for things like *luck, beauty* and *effectiveness*. These nouns do not have a physical form and cannot be touched. **dâai** ได้ can be placed before an abstract noun in order to have a distinct meaning. See Secret 2.

2.1.3 Classifiers

Thai count nouns are called *classifiers*. In English we also have classifiers: *two bottles of milk, head of cattle, a glass of beer*. Perhaps, more accurate term for this type of nouns is "measure words". The difference is that in Thai it is compulsory to use classifiers for all nouns when counting. For example, you cannot say in Thai *two cars*. You must say *a car two vehicles. Vehicle* would be here a classifier in Thai.

2.2 Personal pronouns

Personal pronouns such as *I, he* and *we*. In Thai personal pronouns are used much more and in a wider sense than in English. They refer to age, gender, social status and the context.

2.3 Verbs

2.3.1 Main verb

When **dâai** ได้ is a *main verb*, it means *to get*. See Secrets 1–2.

2.3.2 Helping verb

As a *helping verb* **dâai** ได้ is placed before the main verb or after it. When **dâai** ได้ is placed before the main verb, then it is usually understood as *getting to do* something or *having an opportunity to do* something. After the main verb the meaning is usually *being able to* or *being allowed to do* something. See Secrets 3–6.

2.3.3 Action verbs

Action verbs are verbs that express actions like *to run, to work, to dance*.

2.3.4 State verbs

State verbs describe a state that usually lasts for some time. Some common examples where the state is described are: *to be (He is tall), to have (I have fever), to feel (I feel good)*.

2.3.5 Compound verbs

Compound verbs are used frequently in Thai in the sense that two verbs together form a new meaning. **dâai** ได้ is commonly used as compound verb with many other verbs. When using the compound verb in Thai, the structure is quite tight. This means that we usually cannot put other words between the two verbs.

2.4 Adjectives

2.4.1 Adjectives as adjectives

Adjectives in Thai can be used as *adjectives* as we understand them in English. Adjectives usually answer the question "what kind?". Example: *good, beautiful, happy*. **dâai** ได้ can be placed directly before an adjective in order to make an adjective become an adverb. See Secret 4.

2.4.2 Adjectives as verbs

Adjectives in Thai can be used as *verbs*. In Thai, an adjective can play the role of the English verb *to be*. For the sentence to be complete, all you need is a subject and an adjective. There is no need for any verb as such. A similar structure is not possible in English.

2.4.3 Adjectives as adverbs

Adjectives in Thai can be used as *adverbs*. In Thai adjectives can play the role of an adverb of manner. In Thai when an adjective follows an action verb, "good" becomes *well*, "beautiful" becomes *beautifully* and "slow" becomes *slowly*.

2.5 Adverbs

2.5.1 Adverbs of time

Adverbs of time tell us *when* the action happened, will happen or perhaps that it is happening now. Examples: *yesterday, two days ago, tomorrow, nowadays*. In this book we usually call *adverbs of time "time words"*.

2.5.2 Adverbs of frequency

Adverbs of frequency are used to tell us *how often* the action happens. Examples: *often, regularly, always*. In this book we usually call *adverbs of frequency "time words of frequency"*.

2.5.3 Adverbs of place

Adverbs of place are used to tell us *where* the action happens. Examples: *far, near*.

2.5.4 Adverbs of manner

Adverbs of manner are used to tell us *how and in what way* the action happens. Examples: *slowly, well, gently*. See Secret 4.

2.6 Prepositions

Both Thai and English use *prepositions* like *in, to, above, for.*

2.7 Conjunctions

Conjunction words such as *and, or, but, until* are used to connect two sentences.

> ### 3 Making sentences
>
> In oder to make correct sentences, there are a few basic English terms which may prove helpful to know while learning Thai.

3.1 Simple subject

The *simple subject* is a *noun* or a *pronoun.* It is a person or thing that actively performs the action, the one who is in charge.

3.2 Simple predicate

The *simple predicate* is a *verb*, which describes or tells something about the subject. In Thai an adjective can be both a predicate and an adjective at the same time. No separate verb, as we understand it in English, is needed.

3.3 Object

3.3.1 Direct object

The term *direct object* is used for something which is given.

3.3.2 Indirect object

The term *indirect object* is used for the person to whom the direct object is given.

3.4 Subject-verb-object in the sentence

As you will learn in this book, the subject or the object can be dropped in Thai if understood from the context.

Summary of some useful grammar terms

3.5 Tenses in English

The term *tense* in English is used to describe tenses such as *past, present* and *future*. The semantic meaning of the word *tense* is that the verb changes form when different tenses are used in English.

3.6 Tenses in Thai

The grammar rules in Thai are very straightforward. For instance, the verbs are not conjugated, there are no tenses for verbs, there are no plural forms for nouns and no genders or articles like *a, an* or *the*.

In Thai the *tense* (past, present, future) is made clear by *words*. We conveniently use the English word *tense* when referring to time in Thai. We may say this is a past tense, even though there are no tenses in Thai as such. So, please do not get stuck with the definition of the English word *tense*. After all we are taking about the past, present or future.

3.7 Context

Context can be *verbal* or *social* or both. We use the word *context* in this book in a sense that the speaker takes into account the surroundings in which the conversation takes place and adapts her or his language to suit that context. Therefore, much maybe already understood and not everything needs to be spoken out.

3.8 Short form

We use the *short form* in the sense that when the context is clear, some words, which can be understood from the context, are dropped or left out.

3.9 Idiomatic expressions

Idiomatic expressions are informal ways to convey meanings. An idiomatic phrase may have a different meaning than the words in it. **dâai** ได้ is used in many idiomatic expressions in Thai. Idiomatic expressions give some juice to the expression. See Secrets 7–8.

3.10 Gerund

Gerund is a grammatical term used in English for nouns that are formed from verbs by the ending *-ing* such as *giving*. This kind of noun (gerund) can be a subject or an object in a sentence. In Thai, we form nouns from verbs by placing the prefix **gaan** การ before the verb. **kaan dâai** การ ได้ is translated into English as *getting*.

3.11 Genitive/possessive case

The term *genitive* is used to show *possession*. In English it is usually formed by adding *'s* after a noun or by placing the word *of* before the noun. In Thai the possessive form is created by the word **kɔ̌ɔng** ของ *of*.

3.12 Polite particles

In Thai *polite particles* are used frequently. The most common are **khâ** ค่ะ and **khráp** ครับ. They are not very easy to translate into English. Therefore, we have not given an exact English translation for them in our "word for word" translations. The overall meaning is close to the English word *please*. The polite particles in Thai are used grammatically a different way to the English word *please*. Their usage and "semantic boundaries" are much wider.

4 Other terms

4.1 Schwa

Even though the *schwa* is the most common vowel sound in English, this term is not usually known by native speakers of English language since phonetics is not commonly taught in schools while spelling is. The schwa is a short neutral vowel sound used in English. The sound depends on the consonant it is attached to. A good example is the letter "a" in the word *about*. However, the same letter is pronounced very differently in words such as *can, sad, make, article* where it is not the schwa. The vowel sounds are very clear and distinct in Thai and they cannot be blurred or changed to anything else like schwa in English.

If you are interested in phonetics and how to make correct Thai sounds, you may like to read the book:

22 Secrets of Learning Thai – Complete Guide to Sounds, Tones and Thai Writing System

In Secrets 10 and 13 the first paragragh (daai says:.....) is translated from the following book: Don Miguel Ruiz: The Four Agreements: Practical Guide to Personal Freedom (Toltec Wisdom Book)

Bibliography

Becker, Benjawan Poomsan. Thai for Beginners. Paiboon Publishing, California, 1995.

Becker, Benjawan Poomsan. Thai for Intermediate Learners. Paiboon Publishing, California, 1998.

Becker, Benjawan Poomsan. Thai for Advanced Learners. Paiboon Publishing, California, 2000.

Burusphat Somsonge. Reading and Writing Thai. Institute of Language and Culture for Rural Development, Mahidol University, Bangkok, 2006.

Dhyan, Manik. 22 Secrets of Learning Thai – Complete Guide to Sounds, Tones and Thai Writing System, Dolphin Books, 2014.

Dhyan, Manik. Learning Thai with hâi ให้ Dolphin Books, 2016.

Higbie, James & Thinsan Snea. Thai Reference Grammar: The Structure of Spoken Thai. Orchid Press, Bangkok, 2003.

James, Helen. Thai Reference Grammar. D.K. Editions & Suk's Editions, Bangkok, 2001.

Kanchanawan, Nitaya & Eynon, Matthew J. Learning Thai (A Unique and Practical Approach). Odeon Store, Bangkok, 2005.

Ponmanee, Sriwilai. Speaking Thai for Advanced Learner. Thai Studies Center. Chiang Mai Universtity, Chiang Mai, 2001.

Smyth, David. Thai: An Essential Grammar. Routledge, London and New York, 2002.

Smyth, David. Teach Yourself Thai. Hodder Headline, London, 2003.

22 Secrets of Learning Thai

– Complete Guide to Sounds, Tones and Thai Writing System

ISBN 978-9525572858, 359 pages

Twenty-two Secrets of Learning Thai teaches you all the sounds used in spoken and written Thai. It includes 20 consonant sounds, 18 pure vowel sounds, all special vowels and vowel combinations. It points out the main obstacles for learners, for example which Thai sounds are most difficult for an English speaker to produce. It then gives you handy tips to help overcome these difficulties. Much care has been taken to describe each sound in phonetic as well as in practical terms so that everyone should be able to grasp the correct way to produce Thai sounds.

The book has been designed so that it can be used by all levels of Thai learners. It contains a special exercise section, which teaches you in a step by step manner how to learn to read Thai script. At the same time all the Thai tone rules are taught in theory and practice. The student will get to know the most common Thai consonant symbols as well as rare symbols mostly borrowed from Indic languages, Pali and Sanskrit.

This book is also available in two seperates books as follows:

Basic Sounds of the Thai Language, Book I
(Secrets 1-15 ISBN 978-9526651323, 182 pages)

Advanced Sounds of the Thai Language, Book II
(Secrets 16-22 ISBN 978-9526651330, 178 pages)

22 Secrets of Learning Thai

– *Learning Thai with hâi* ให้
ISBN 978-9526651156, 296 pages

hâi ให้, along with words like dâai ได้, lέεu แล้ว and kɔ̂ɔ ก็, is one of the most important words in the Thai language.

When speaking Thai, it is important to understand the correct usage of the verb hâi ให้ in everyday speech.

One simple way to use the verb hâi ให้ is *to give something to someone*. It is used in a similar manner as the English verb *to give*.

In addition, hâi ให้ is used as a causative verb which has several different meanings depending on the situation, and the way it is spoken. It can be translated into English as *to let, to allow, to make* and even *to order* or *to force someone to do something*.

In some situations hâi ให้ is better translated into English as the preposition *for*, as in *for you, for me*, etc. It is also often used in idiomatic phrases where it carries no meaning itself but denotes only the sense of a command.

Thais use the verb hâi ให้ in an intuitive way in a variety of situations in order to express feelings, wishes, commands and nuances of meaning while communicating with each other every day.

If you learn this word well, you will be rewarded.

22 Secrets of Learning Thai

– *Learning Thai Tenses with dâai* ได้

Book II, Secrets 15–22

ISBN 978-9526651408 , 278 pages

Whether you are a beginner or an advanced learner, you will surely want to learn to speak Thai fluently. In order to do this, it is vital to use time words and tense markers correctly.

The English term *tense* is also a handy way to talk about past, present and future activities in Thai, even though there are no *tenses* as such in the Thai language. When compared to English, Thai tenses are expressed very differently.

It is often said that dâai ได้ denotes a past tense. However, it would be better not to think of dâai ได้ as the past tense marker since it can also be used to refer to present or future events.

To help you speak Thai fluently the Book II includes:
- complete and informative written examples
- audio spoken by native speakers
- highlights and explanations of dâai's ได้ usage
- sections of simple and easy to understand advice
- useful hints and tips on dâai ได้ and the spoken Thai language

Books I and II complement each other. However, each book has a different focus. In Book I, Secrets 1–14, we introduced dâai ได้ and explained where it should be placed in sentences. dâai ได้ has several grammatical functions; hence, it also has several meanings depending on the context. In Book II, Secrets 15–22, we focus on tenses.

Have fun while you study them both; then, you will understand how Thais express themselves in everyday life!

Learning Thai Quickly and Easily

with Original Thai Words

ISBN 978-9526651439, 320 pages

Do you want to learn to speak Thai as naturally as Thais do? Thai is not as difficult as you may think! If you follow the guidelines of this book, you will acquire a basic knowledge of the language in just a few weeks.

Students, usually, face several obstacles when studying Thai. In this book, we shall explain clearly what these obstacles are and how to overcome them. We shall also point out what you need to know and what you may ignore when learning to speak Thai. This will ensure your time and effort is focused on the things that really matter. You will be in a position to make an informed decision on how to proceed and deepen your language skills.

We use a simple and direct method which is easy to comprehend. You don't have to master the complex Thai writing system in order to speak Thai fluently. In this book, we concentrate on "original Thai words" which form a very important part of the Thai vocabulary and are used by Thais every day in conversation.

The book is designed in such a way that it can be used by both beginners and by those who have already reached intermediate level.

Included are:
- written examples and sentences
- audio spoken by native speakers
- highlights, explanations and examples on "how the language works"
- simple and easy to understand advice
- hints and tips on spoken Thai language
- "Take it further" section which includes many more tips on how to proceed with your studies

Now, you can tell all your friends that learning Thai can be easy. Read this book and you will discover how!

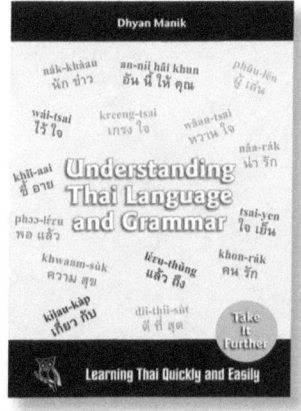

Learning Thai Quickly and Easily

Understanding Thai Language and Grammar – Take It Further

ISBN 978-9526651460, 264 pages

Undertanding the structure and grammar of the Thai languge is very important since it may differ considerably from your own language

Included are:

- Original Thai words compared to foreign origin words
- Personal pronouns and family members
- Days, weeks, months, seasons and numbers
- Telling time – 24-hour clock compared to the Thai style
- Foods, drinks and spices
- Travelling, places, buildings and countries of the world
- Names of animals and insects
- Health words and personal items
- Adjectives, adverbs and verbs
- Thai question words, prepositions and conjunction words
- Classifiers and prefixes
- tsai ใจ heart -word
- Summary of the Thai tenses
- Words of wisdom

This book has been designed to be used as a compliment to the book "Learning Thai with Original Thai Words". It can be used, however, with any other Thai learning book.

Coming books:

22 Secrets of Learning Thai:

- Learning Thai Tenses with lɛ́ɛu แล้ว
  (coming 2023 ISBN 978-9526651446)
- Learning Thai with kɔ̂ɔ ก็
  (coming 2025 ISBN 978-9526651453)

Learning Thai Quickly and Easily:

- Learning Thai with English Words
  (coming 2024 ISBN 978-9526651347)
- Learning Thai with Foreign Words
  Pali, Sanskrit, Khmer, Chinese...
  (coming 2026 ISBN 978-9526651477)

Our books can be obtained from the following bookshops in Thailand:

DK today
www.dktoday.co.th

Asia Books
www.asiabooks.com

Kinokuniya
www.kinokuniya.com

Chulalongkorn University Book Center
www.chulabook.com

Thammasat University Bookstore
www.bookstore.tu.ac.th

Chiang Mai University Bookstore
http://www.cmubook.com

Naiin Bookstore
www.naiin.com

Audio spoken in MP3 format by native speakers can be loaded from the following address:

www.thaibooks.net

Thai voice: Ms. Waree Singhanart
English voice: Mr. Mark Harris

For more information

Publisher:

www.dolphinbooks.org
info@dolphinbooks.org

www.thaibooks.net
www.facebook.com/22Secrets

www.ingramcontent.com/pod-product-compliance
Lightning Source LLC
LaVergne TN
LVHW091628070526
838199LV00044B/985